Sharing Writing

Peer Response Groups
in English Classes

Sharing Writing

Peer Response Groups in English Classes

KAREN SPEAR

University of Utah

BOYNTON/COOK PUBLISHERS
HEINEMANN
PORTSMOUTH, NH

Boynton/Cook Publishers
A Division of
Heinemann Educational Books Inc.
70 Court Street, Portsmouth, NH 03801

Printed in the United States of America

89 90 91 10 9 8 7 6 5 4 3 2

Library of Congress Cataloging-in-Publication Data

Spear, Karen I.
    Sharing writing / by Karen Spear.
        p.   cm.
    ISBN 0-86709-189-4
    1. English language—Composition and exercises—Study and
teaching—United States. 2. Group work in education. 3. Language
arts (Secondary)—United States. 4. Language arts (Higher)—United
States.   I. Title
LB1631.S66   1987
808'.042'071173—dc19   87–23067
                                                                CIP

"Concealed Colors," "STARS," "Perceiving Relations," "Kinships and Associations," "The Frugal Woman," "Sound and Meaning," "Common Denominators," "Word Chains," "Metaphorical Thinking," and "Pairs" from Creative Growth Games, *copyright 1977 by Eugene Raudsepp and George P. Hughs, Jr., is reprinted by permission of The Berkley Publishing Group.*

Acknowledgments

It should come as no surprise that a book about sharing writing has benefited greatly from the listening, encouragement, and feedback of others. Three readers, in particular, became my response group and showed me the best of what peer readers can do for a writer: William Strong, who by now has a drawerful of drafts but who has always been willing to read and respond to one more version; Kenneth Eble, who provided very substantive advice about structuring the manuscript and improving on its practical side; and Peter Stillman, who became more of a writing partner and teacher than an editor. Their commitment to the project and their encouragement were as essential as the guidance they so generously provided.

I am also grateful to Francine Danis for sharing transcripts she prepared of response groups in her own classes. Thanks are due as well to Lisa Barker and Connie Keuffel for the hours they spent on careful preparation of the manuscript.

Deep appreciation goes to my husband, Terry Bacon, for his adamant belief that the project should be more extensive than I initially envisioned. Finally, I gratefully acknowledge the many teachers in Utah's public schools who have consistently guided me by reacting thoughtfully to my ideas, by sharing their own classroom experiences, and by asking me the hard questions about how to make response groups work.

Preface

One of the most perplexing gaps between theory and practice in teaching writing is the use of peer response groups. In theory, response groups provide an audience and purpose, making writing a genuine act of communication. Some of the best minds in the discipline—James Moffett, Ken Macrorie, Peter Elbow, Kenneth Bruffee, to name a few—have persuasively described groups' many intimate ties with writing and learning processes. As a result, few serious teachers of writing today can remain unimpressed by the powerful potential of having students share their thoughts and drafts.

In practice, though, teachers from elementary school through college often regard group work with anything from mild reservation to outright frustration. Students' reactions vary. Many enjoy working in groups, but sometimes more for their social opportunities than academic ones. Other students, convinced they can learn only from teachers, resent the time that groups take away from direct instruction. Nevertheless, study after study shows that when response groups do "work," students' learning becomes richer, more exciting, and more long lasting than it does under teacher-centered conditions.

This book explores the gap between theory and practice in the use of response groups. It provides a detailed analysis of students' problems in writing groups and offers a variety of techniques and suggestions to complement writing development and group interaction. The work grows out of my thesis that students must learn the interpersonal skills that make fruitful discussion of writing possible. Effective response groups result from knowledge and practice, not just luck. My approach rests on three assumptions:

- By nature, composing is an interpersonal process.
- Students' problems with writing parallel their problems with interacting in groups.
- When students learn how to participate in groups *along with* how to write, writing and learning become closely connected in the dynamic sense of exploring, discovering, and shaping meaning that we have come to associate with composing.

This book is designed primarily for teachers of writing in secondary and higher education. We recognize that during this period, writing is integral to education because of its value in stimulating the higher cognitive functions. For the same reason, I maintain that the development of skills in peer interaction should accompany writing instruction. Mature group discussion also demands the operation of higher orders of thinking. However, neither mature writing nor mature group discussion just happens. Both result from students' having continued and meaningful opportunities for practice, aided by the coaching and direct instruction that informed teachers provide. The emphasis on continued and meaningful opportunities is essential because there is every reason to believe that just as writing deteriorates in the face of increasingly complex tasks, so does group interaction come unraveled as students are confronted by new and ever more challenging intellectual demands.

Accordingly, I take a very hard look at student interaction in response groups to provide a critical analysis of the benefits as well as the difficulties of sharing writing. My concern is not just with the techniques of creating effective writing groups, but with the place of peer interaction in the larger development of writing and learning. Too many teachers take a stab at using groups only to become disappointed, frustrated, and sometimes embittered when students fail to live up to their expectations. Without trying to discourage or to work at the apparent cross purpose of criticizing groups' effectiveness while promoting their use, I nevertheless confront the very real problems students experience in response groups. This way I hope teachers of writing will be able to make informed use of peer response groups so their success can be far less serendipitous than is often the case.

My analysis is based on an eclectic, interdisciplinary blend of methods and resources. My primary research comes from observation of peer response groups from junior high students to upper division undergraduates, along with an analysis of group transcripts. I have also drawn on research from a variety of fields: composition theory, learning theory, information theory, psychotherapy, group process, and literature on student development. This analysis occupies Part I, *Challenges of Peer Response Groups.*

Based on this analysis, Part II, *Developing Productive Peer Response Groups*, is devoted to practical application. Readers who are primarily interested in how-to may want to start with this section, although that's a little like drawing up blueprints without having visited the building site—possible but perhaps not entirely desirable.

I offer two kinds of application in Part II. More immediately, there is a wealth of specific classroom activities for starting, maintaining, and improving peer response groups. Less immediate, but still essential, is somewhat more theoretical background on the nature of reading, listening, and giving feedback in response groups—material necessary for teachers to understand and convey to students.

Chapter 6 establishes a framework for Part II by presenting and analyzing a successful revision session. The participants' commentary on their session shows that students themselves can become a valuable resource for examining and improving the process. Chapter 7 shows how to start a peer-centered writing class so that the relations among the writing, thinking, and interacting in groups are clarified. Chapter 8 takes up the problem of helping students develop effective reading strategies for working with peer texts. Then, chapters 9 and 10 develop a continuum for peer interaction from listening to providing feedback. This continuum parallels the continuum in composing from generating ideas and drafting to revising and editing. Chapter 11 offers a menu of group activities as a troubleshooting guide for a variety of group problems. These chapters offer more suggestions than any one teacher could use. They do, however, provide ideas for change ranging from relatively minor teaching strategies to large-scale curriculum design.

My aim throughout the book has been to blend theoretical issues with practical considerations, the why alongside the how. Methods books and lesson plans seem of little value without a comprehensive understanding of why the methods work (or should work). Further, like the many formulaic guides that so regularly fail to teach students to write or teachers to teach, lists of methods or teaching suggestions alone tend to shortcut or obscure the problem in the rush to provide a solution. On the other hand, the analysis and suggestions I have provided should serve as springboards for individual teachers to make adaptations, develop ideas of their own, and implement techniques in their own ways.

Benjamin Franklin's observations at the signing of the U.S. Constitution—a collaborative document if ever there was one—give one of the most realistic assessments of the power and perils of the response-group process:

> I agree to this Constitution with all its faults, if they are such, because . . . I doubt whether any other convention . . . may be able to make a better Constitution. For when you assemble a number of men to have the advantage of their joint wisdom, you inevitably assemble with those men all their prejudices, their passions, their errors of opinion, their local interests and their selfish views. From such an assembly can a perfect production be expected? It therefore astonishes me, Sir, to find this system approaching so near to perfection as it does. . . . Thus I consent, Sir, to this Constitution because I expect no better, and because I am not sure that it is not the best.
>
> September 17, 1787

Like Franklin, I can find no better way to help students learn to write, and I am not sure that it is not the best.

Contents

Sharing Writing

Peer Response Groups
in English Classes

PART I

Challenges of
Peer Response Groups

1

The Composing Process and the Interpersonal Process

Education, in order to accomplish its ends both for the individual
learner and for society, must be based upon experience—which is
always the actual life experience of some individual.

—John Dewey
Experience and Education
1938

Popular stereotypes depict writing as a lonely act. We envision the
writer scribbling by candlelight in a chilly garret or, less romantically, clicking
away at a computer terminal with only the blinking cursor for a friend. The
isolation and tedium associated with these images color people's attitudes
toward writing; they are not pleasant prospects. Despite these familiar images,
writing is really a lively communal activity. The permanence of written texts
allows people to share something of themselves and their ideas. Writing is
thought made palpable, part of a social dialectic that enables us to check our
perceptions against others', develop our ideas, modify and continue our
thinking.

The communal features of writing are even more significant when we
consider not written products but the process of writing. Whenever writers
seek responses from others by verbalizing ideas or sharing drafts, the process
of writing becomes a social one. Sharing allows writers to hear what their
ideas sound like and to solicit feedback as they continue to think about a
topic, draft, or revise. The verbal and nonverbal feedback they receive contributes to the evolution of ideas. Even the most private writing is shaped by
our social interactions—whether as a stimulus for writing or an imagined
scenario in our minds. Like many a diary entry or letter that goes unsent, this
writing often says privately what one wishes to but cannot say publicly.
Sometimes such writing works cathartically; sometimes it helps us prepare for
real exchanges—oral or written—with others.

Even in its most subtle origins, the process of writing has communal
roots. It probably derives from what Vygotsky called "inner speech," the

3

stream of language that runs through our minds, reflecting external language heard in conversation. At the other extreme, the most public writing—business and educational reports, government documents, corporate publications—is often done collaboratively: a pair or even a team of writers generates ideas, then writes and revises their text. The process is recursive: talking and drafting, talking and revising, talking and editing.

These examples, however, concern "real" writing—the writing people do for reasons of their own usually outside the context of school. School writing easily slips into a different category. Too frequently it is writing done not to inform or persuade or entertain or any of the other functions real writing serves, but usually to measure up, to qualify, to prove oneself as a student, perhaps as a student-writer, but not usually just as a writer, not just as a person with something worthwhile to say. And it is written for an audience that usually responds to it from a mental checklist of criteria, registering correctness, organization, diction, coverage and quality of content, and the like—someone who reads out of a professional obligation, but usually not to be personally affected or informed by the text. Janet Emig thus concluded from her study of twelfth grade writers that school writing "is a limited, and limiting experience."[1]

The context of school writing differs from that of "real" writing and potentially distorts it. Out of this awareness, many teachers have been turning increasingly toward small group interaction to help students experience the problems of audience and purpose as they affect writers in actual writing situations. Ideally, sharing ideas and drafts with peers makes regular and disciplined practice of what many writers do routinely: they conceive subject and purpose in terms of an audience, develop their ideas and their presentation accordingly, and check their progress at various points with some other person. Sometimes that person is part of the intended audience, but more often it is someone who knows the audience or who can anticipate it and, most important, someone whose opinion is valued and trusted.

In writing classes, group interaction reinforces the notion that writing is not just what you end up with but the activities you undertake in creating it: the process as well as the product. Thus group interaction protentially helps to offset the artificiality of a writing class by enlarging the reading audience, introducing problems of genuine communication, supplying multiple perspectives and points of view, and modifying the teacher's many complex roles as instigator, helper, critic, audience, and evaluator.

Peer Interaction Throughout the Composing Process

Sharing is valuable throughout the composing process. The emphasis in recent years on heuristic procedures for individual writers has tended to overshadow what is perhaps the more common practice among experienced writers:

exchanging, developing, and exploring ideas collaboratively. Sharing thought orally prior to writing helps to shape and test thought; the tentativeness of oral language allows the writer to "rehearse" ideas verbally: to express them orally and "hear" their sound and sense before the more substantial commitment of words on paper. Subsequently, sharing drafts with peers serves to maintain their tentative status as unfinished thinking. Peer interaction at this stage helps not just to confirm the effectiveness of what has been written but, ideally at least, to prolong invention.

Finally, sharing revisions with peers functions almost as a final dress rehearsal, giving writers, like actors, the opportunity to review their production for previously undetected flaws or shortcomings, to witness it as an actual audience would, and to make the stylistic modifications that bring writer and reader together. At this stage, too, emerge some of the most tangible benefits for teachers of sharing writing. Despite our intentions to read students' texts for content, structure, logic, quality of thought and the like, we still stumble over obstacles of sentence structure, spelling, punctuation, and grammar.[2] Although peer review of texts has the potential to achieve much more, students should at the very least become responsible for editing, proofreading, and correcting their peers' texts.

It is important to emphasize, too, that peer review in writing classes need not mean that students write solely for each other. In fact, to the extent that peer readers must imagine and anticipate an intended audience's response to a text, the process of sharing writing can be equally instructive to readers as well as writers. Asking peer readers to read from a perspective other than their own can do as much to overcome students' egocentricity as can writing itself. (Chapters 3 and 8 explore peers' reading processes in more detail.)

Employed throughout the composing process, group learning techniques represent a commitment to more than the student writer's immediate needs to produce successful or effective texts. In his extremely practical guide to small-group writing instruction, Thom Hawkins identifies the personal, social, and pedagogical goals of group learning that distinguish it from teacher-centered situations:

1. Students can take responsibility for their own learning in the classroom, just as they often do outside the classroom.
2. Working in small groups . . . encourages active participation in the learning process by all students.
3. During small-group work in the classroom, the most effective role for the teacher is to facilitate learning by questioning, listening, and observing.[3]

These goals are more than procedural; they represent a philosophy of education concerned with what people learn and, more importantly, how they learn it. Group learning transcends the cliché of making students responsible for their own learning. In the group situation, "responsibility" means that learning becomes operational not simply receptive, purposive not simply reactive. Group learning can provide the foundation that John Dewey insisted was essential to all learning: "the formation of purposes which direct [the student's] activities in the learning process." [4] Working collaboratively, students must define problems for themselves and critically explore solutions; in so doing they practice crucial skills in listening, talking, and reading; in generating ideas, generalizing, abstracting, debating; and above all in assessing their own performance. In short, group learning in the writing process allows students direct access to the processes of inquiry and discovery as they naturally occur—processes that oftentimes students only hear about at second or third hand from their teachers.[5]

Writing groups are particularly relevant to achieving these more general aims. People often write to explore a problem and through writing chart that exploration, uniquely opening to writer and readers alike a window on the processes of problem-solving and problem-finding. In this respect, writing groups can do more than produce effective or correct texts. More important, they engage writers in the communal enterprises of knowing and sharing what is known. As Kenneth Bruffee explains it, students sharing each other's writing learn "to ask where their peers are coming from as the author of a given essay and where they hope to go with the piece. Thus, writing groups, whether formal or informal, help students learn how writers behave and to become helpful and productive members of the community of effective writers."[6]

Writers here are more than transcribers, but as we now are increasingly coming to understand, they are originators of meaning. Heady stuff indeed, but any child who asks a parent to look over an essay, any college student who talks out ideas with a dormmate, or any professional who buttonholes a colleague saying, "Hey Barbara, what do you think about this?" or delivers an exploratory paper at a professional meeting is engaging in writing as a way of knowing.

The Rhetoric of Peer Instruction

I am suggesting, then, that composing and peer instruction are really two sides of the same rhetorical coin. To ignore or overlook the rhetorical dimension of either is to blunt the possibilities of both. Talking, like writing, necessitates audience and purpose, discovery and "arrangement." It provides the added advantage of instant response and feedback. Thus, the act of talking is a process of discovering, articulating, and clarifying meaning based on the flow of verbal and non-verbal cues the interaction generates. With the exception of so many college classrooms and papers delivered at professional conferences, talking is not a static act of oral transcription from mind to mouth or from speaker to listener, any more than writing is simply written transcription. Both involve the more evolutionary, interpersonal processes of composing, reinventing, and revising.

The real value of peer-centered writing instruction is that it develops the rhetorical dimension of both oral and written discourse while emphasizing the changing, dynamic features of writing as a process. We characterize as "experienced" writers who have learned to capitalize on the evolving, even mercurial nature of composing; inexperienced writers seem less tolerant of flux, more resistant to the notions of sowing and cultivating ideas. Experienced writers discover their own purposes and anticipate their own audiences; less experienced writers, especially in school, seem unable to think beyond what has been reinforced for them by longstanding academic conventions.[7] According to these conventions, the purpose for writing is to do the teacher's assignment; the writer's role is narrowly conceived as that of student; the audience is the teacher; the goal is to transcribe a preconceived thesis in a form and style consistent with that reader's preconceived standards. Even many adults who avoid, even despise, writing seem to do so because they cannot break their associations of writing with school, bound up as these associations are in feelings of frustration, failure, and purposelessness.

Peer interaction, because its rhetorical features are inherently more realistic and more immediate, has the capacity to keep these self-defeating associations from forming. Group discussion provides opportunities throughout the composing process for novice writers to behave like their more experienced counterparts.

However, as the literature on group process demonstrates, successful groups are fragile things indeed. Groups assume a life of their own; in the Gestalt sense, a group is not just more than but also different from the sum of its members. In view of the complexities of group process and the inexpeience of the student writers, it is perhaps more surprising when peer interaction groups do work than when they don't. A number of issues combine to make peer discussion of writing a sometimes fruitless endeavor: a tradition of teacher-centered education, students' genuine puzzlement over what constitutes quality in writing and thinking, suspicion about the teacher's motives, along with self-consciousness, self-doubt, and timidity.

Despite their rich potential, peer response groups don't work just because we think they should—any more than liver tastes good just because it's supposed to be good for us. Students are no more expert at contributing productively to groups than they are at writing. And teachers can no more expect them to write well without instruction than to discuss writing effectively without help. In fact, given the rhetorical similarities of writing and discussing writing, many student shortcomings manifest in one medium are also reflected in the other—shortcomings in discovering ideas, developing and elaborating thoughts, reading, reviewing and responding critically, perceiving connections, exploring alternative organizations. Though directed toward somewhat different outcomes, the group movement of the past two decades and the peer-centered writing class of today share many of the same concerns: the need for participants to explore the limitations of their own points of view, to discover and articulate significant feelings and ideas, and to experience the effects of their perceptions, behavior, and statements on others.

If student groups are to realize the potential I have been outlining, teachers must, as Gorman emphasizes in *Teachers and Learners,* accept the responsibility for teaching students how to communicate in a group setting. What for most students is a radical change in the classroom medium must be accompanied by instruction in how to use that new medium.[8] In their work on *Small Group Teaching,* Sharan and Sharan echo this theme: "Procedures and skills for cooperative learning are acquired with experience; they are not natural endowments."[9] Bruffee, too, emphasizes the importance of structured group experiences for writing groups, observing that "without guidance, peer influence can have a conservative effect potentially detrimental to intellectual growth."[10] I can hear the frustration in the writing teacher's voice now: "First you tell me that groups are essential to learning how to write; then you say students don't know how to work in groups. I don't have enough time to teach them to write; you expect me to teach group process, too? I'm a writing teacher, not a psychologist."

These are legitimate frustrations. However, they stem from preconceptions that isolate one skill from another, one discipline from another. A collaborative model of writing is necessarily holistic and interdisciplinary. Collaborative writing instruction depends upon two related assumptions on the teacher's part: (1) the nature of writing as an epistemological process and (2) the place of skill development and its role in the larger learning process. Let me explain these assumptions to show how collaborative writing can weave together students' development as learners and writers.

Writing, Talking, and Knowing

First, as we have come increasingly to recognize in the last ten years, writing as a process includes a complex array of epistemological and interpersonal issues ranging from how and what one comes to know to expressing and communicating what is known.[11] From this perspective, writing is emerging from its formerly limited role in the curriculum as a testing instrument to become a powerful tool in helping students and teachers alike understand and improve the learning process. The writing-across-the-curriculum movement, an effort to introduce writing as the medium of learning in all disciplines, is the most important consequence of this broader understanding of the function of writing, and a topic I will take up in more detail below.

Integrating Skill Development with Course Content to Improve Learning

The second assumption is similarly holistic. With public attention riveted during the late 70's on the "literacy crisis," writing instruction has for the most part emerged as a worthwhile academic endeavor. However, for many minds it still occupies an ambiguous gray area between the remedial zone of basic skills and the upper reaches of intellectual inquiry. To the extent that it is regarded as a basic skill rather than a "meta-skill," teachers in disciplines including English find that writing instruction interferes with their primary interest in covering content, and they are tempted to relegate writing to specialists of the sort that teach other, often remedial matters such as study skills, test-taking, or reading.[12] It is equally tempting to regard group interaction as a similar set of skills that should be taught elsewhere because developing them likewise takes time away from the central task of covering subject matter.

In "Developing Student Skills and Abilities," Clark Bouton and Beryl Rice sum up the problems for teaching and learning from this unfortunate tendency first to define skills pejoratively and then to isolate them from course content. Although they are primarily concerned with higher education, their comments seem equally relevant to all levels of teaching:

> The prevalent response to students' deficiencies in academic skills has been to demand more skills courses. For their part, teachers attempt to get the content of their courses across to students in ways that reduce the demands on students' skills. This response is self-defeating. Skills do not exist in the abstract, and students cannot learn a skill, such as writing, much less thinking, in one or two skills courses. However, both by avoiding their share of the responsibility for developing students' skills and by using teaching methods that attempt to compensate for students' low level of skills, teachers deprive students of the chance to develop needed skills. Given the training that college [and secondary] teachers receive and the fragmentation of the curriculum into specialized subject matters, the teacher is primarily concerned with covering the material of a course, and the development of skills seems to belong either to other specialists or to no one in particular.[13]

Bouton and Rice contend that the integration of skills with content not only results in the joint development of higher and lower order skills but also vastly improves students' mastery of course content. In writing classes—or classes that use writing—the reciprocity of composition and group interaction similarly improves learning.

However, many teachers complain that achieving this kind of integration, logical and aesthetically pleasing as it is in theory, is well nigh impossible in practice. Group learning seems particularly vulnerable to this complaint. Teachers must not only design and sequence the content of group assignments; they must also account for group process. However, I'll argue throughout this book that integrating skills with content, or skills with skills, is only problematic when the two are viewed as separate and mutually exclusive. When skills and content are considered not just as complementary but as integrated, we are no longer in the frustrating if not impossible dilemma of stealing time from one task to undertake another.

Peer Response and Writing Across the Curriculum

As I've suggested, the natural outcome of this marriage of skills and content is the writing-across-the-curriculum movement—an effort not to introduce but to clarify the nature of writing as a central component of learning in all disciplines. Although a long time coming, the writing-across-the-curriculum movement is a healthy and sophisticated countermeasure throughout secondary and higher education to the simplistic, back-to-basics thinking that has been the more visible response to "the literacy crisis."

Writing across the curriculum has grown out of three principles: first, that English teachers cannot be solely responsible for formal instruction in writing or for the quality of students' writing; second, that writing, because it is fundamental to the thinking and learning processes associated with any subject, should figure prominently in the teaching of all disciplines; third, that since writing is the standard form of communication in many of the occupations for which schools prepare students, graduates must know how to communicate in writing within a given field. Once we accept these principles, it follows that we expect more writing of students and demand that it be of higher quality and greater conceptual maturity than before. Collaborative learning and peer response groups have not been explicitly tied to writing across the curriculum. However, if sharing writing is, by definition, central to the writing process, we cannot overlook the strongly implicit connections.

Fundamentally, writing across the curriculum indicates a turning away in schools from narrowly defined careerism and a rediscovery of the liberal education ideal in which the separate parts of the curriculum are bound together by a common concern for written expression and the critical intelligence that writing represents. Writing across the curriculum originated in higher education, where school-wide programs such as those at Beaver College, Montana State University, University of Michigan, UCLA, and others indicate remarkable energy and commitment. Teachers and administrators throughout higher education have shown considerable enthusiasm and largesse in embracing the principles of writing across the curriculum by developing new, discipline-specific courses in writing, by altering requirements within the major to accommodate writing requirements, and even by trading off valuable research time to engage in extended workshops and seminars on writing—a preparation for becoming more active in cultivating students' writing abilities in all disciplines.

Recently, secondary education has also been influenced by this movement—not just because secondary schools typically follow the lead of the colleges but because with the renewed emphasis on quality in public education there is an insistence that writing is the foremost tool for clarifying and organizing thinking and learning. For instance, the Carnegie Foundation report, *High School,* gives writing across the curriculum considerable impetus. Ernest Boyer calls literacy "the essential tool" and is unequivocal in asserting that spoken and written language must be the cornerstone of the secondary curriculum:

> The first curriculum priority is language. . . . Language provides the connecting tissue that binds society together, allowing us to express feelings and ideas, and powerfully influence the attitudes of others. It is the most essential tool for learning. We recommend that high schools help all students develop the capacity to think critically and communicate effectively through the written and spoken word.[14]

So far, however, many of our efforts to connect writing and learning have focused on faculty and administration, less directly on students. To implement writing across the curriculum, we are relying on traditional solutions to academic problems—better trained teachers, more courses, more money. Equally important is preparing students to live up to the more rigorous demands we intend to place on them. To do so, we need to incorporate disciplined training in the techniques of sharing and developing writing collaboratively with the rest of our efforts to integrate writing into the curriculum.

The Role of Introductory Writing Instruction

Once English teachers relinquish the burden for all writing instruction—instruction often limited to a single course or an occasional unit in high school—they can begin to devote more serious attention to making early writing instruction truly introductory. Rather than designing units or courses that try to be everything to everybody, they can limit the goals and content of introductory writing, making it more intensive and less extensive, confident that instruction will continue in other courses and subject areas. With this redefinition, the English teacher's role also gains in depth what it loses in breadth. We assume the added responsibility of teaching students how to learn from one another in English classes as in other classes—a responsibility in which we account for "rhetoric" in its truest sense. Other disciplines can build upon this foundation just as they will continue to have a role in students' writing development. By coupling writing development with group development, teachers of all disciplines can begin to use writing in the broad social and conceptual context that the Carnegie Foundation finds so essential.

Peer Interaction in the Learning Process

Numerous essays have detailed the important contribution of writing to the learning process, particularly modes of writing not usually included in courses outside English. Art Young's essay on the poetic function of writing for personalizing learning and clarifying values,[15] and James Kalmbach and William Powers' essay on narrative writing[16] suggest the significance of poetic and narrative forms for internalizing new ideas and forging connections between the old and the new. Toby Fulwiler's work on journal writing likewise presents useful and convincing illustrations of how the self-expressive process of exploring ideas in a journal enhances learning in and out of class.[17]

Other scholars, concerned that the sheer volume of increased student writing will intimidate teachers in other disciplines from fully integrating writing into their teaching, have explored alternative assignment types whose brevity and ease of evaluation allow teachers to maintain their primary emphasis on covering content while linking writing to the learning process. Their research is suggesting that teachers who use such assignments are not just doing what is morally good. For instance, John Bean, Dean Drenk, and F. D. Lee's research on "microthemes" indicates that students who regularly write even such brief pieces as these master course content more fully than those who don't.[18] Still more recently, Stephen Tchudi, under the sponsorship of the National Education Association, has begun to apply these findings more directly to teaching in middle school, junio and senior high.[19]

All these approaches, significant as they are in advocating and stimulating writing across the curriculum, give us part but not all of the picture. They don't really account for the inventing, drafting, and revising activities that produce finished texts. These activities, necessary as most teachers will concede they are for writing well, are nevertheless most at odds with the constraints of time and professional preparation felt by teachers outside English. No matter how committed teachers may be to the idea of writing across the curriculum, the reality is that many are understandably reluctant to devote extensive class time to instructing students in drafting and revising texts.

The use of peer response groups—requiring *students* to continue using and developing the interaction and composing skills learned in their preliminary writing courses—can shift much of the responsibility for writing across the curriculum to the students themselves. Although teachers in the disciplines still need to understand how to design assignments according to realistic cognitive and rhetorical dimensions and how to structure and supervise peer group activities, they will serve more comfortably as managers or facilitators rather than as teachers of writing. Once students have come to accept the communal nature of writing and have developed the fundamentals of sharing it, much of their interaction can take place outside the classroom. This offers the benefit of stimulating a school's social and intellectual milieu and gives the entire curriculum a coherence of method and purpose.

The use of peer response groups in writing across the curriculum has the added advantage of helping the whole faculty explore possibilities for collaborative learning, particularly for collaborative projects to complement individual work. Group learning might then become the rule rather than the exception, genuinely embedding writing into what Neil Postman and Charles Weingartner would call the "languaging" processes of thinking and learning about any subject[20] and better preparing students for the collaborative obligations that await them in their professional lives.

Summing up the role of discourse in liberal education, Marshall Gregory suggests the central function of oral and written interaction to the ideals of teaching embodied in the liberal education tradition. As the form of learning properly devoted to cultivating "virtuous action," liberal education links the institutional needs of educating with students' "real world" needs of using what they have learned. For Gregory this connection occurs through spoken and written interaction—what he calls "discourse":

> The most helpful activity we can engage in is *discourse*, the activity of testing and being tested in intricate and sustained communal dance. Discourse—that ancient activity of challenging each other's opinions because we want to know the truth of things, and the attempt to build seaworthy arguments that will not founder in the tempests of controvesry—is the most civilizing activity we can engage in. It is not in itself virtue, and it is no guarantee of virtue, but it does, so to speak, put us in the way of virtue, for it forces us into the kinds of confrontations that make it difficult . . . to maintain the pretenses and evasions by which we hide the truth about ourselves from ourselves. Good hard discourse smokes out our inconsistencies and self-serving justifications, and, if approached in the right spirit, teaches us better than any other activity to know ourselves.[21]

Discourse, in other words, is the cement of liberal learning. Whether confined to a particular program or expressed as the underlying philosophy of undergraduate and even secondary education, discourse is the liberalizing force that sustains the process and nourishes the product of learning across the curriculum. As Gregory's comments suggest, discourse reflects a continuous interplay, the "dance" of students in their language activities, from spoken to written language and back again. Potentially, it cements the secular aims of career preparation with the liberal-humanist tradition of right thought and moral action.

Collaborative Writing and the Professional World

Writing through peer collaboration does not just satisfy educational ideals, although that function is in itself compelling. Knowing how to collaborate with peers, especially on writing projects, is perhaps the most neglected yet essential feature of preparation for professional life. The lifeblood of a corporation or government agency is in the documents it produces. These documents comprise its history, its policies, its plans, its future. Given the importance of an organization's documents, as well as the complexity of the subject matter they treat, a single author is almost *never* entrusted with sole responsibility either for researching or preparing a written or oral report. Writing and collaboration are, in practice, the same thing.

In the Forest Service, for example, "ID [interdisciplinary] teams" composed of members representing a variety of fields—a forester, a wildlife biologist, a geologist, a hydrologist, an archeologist, an economist, a soils expert—work together to produce environmental statements or environmental assessments (a practice that should suggest to educators the continued need to explore opportunities for interdisciplinary teaching and learning).

Group interaction is also the rule in the private sector. The oil industry, for example, functions almost entirely by committee both in preparing proposals and reports and in making corporate decisions. Not only are the research and writing of documents collaborative efforts, the presentation of proposals to management—which in turn operates in committees—are group efforts as well. Corporate decisions, too, come in the form of collaborative, written statements.

The point is that if we don't incorporate collaborative learning, especially in writing, into teaching practices at all levels, we give students unrealistic or downright incorrect pictures of what professional life is all about, along with what constitutes intellectual life generally. In *The Lives of a Cell,* Lewis Thomas makes much the same point about scientific inquiry as a process of oral and written collaboration:

> It is fascinating that the word "explore" does not apply to the searching aspect of the activity, but has its origins in the sounds we make while engaged in it. We like to think of exploring in science as a lonely, meditative business, and so it is in the first stages, but always, sooner or later, before the enterprise reaches completion, as we explore, we call to each other, communicate, publish, send letters to the editor, present papers, cry out on finding.[22]

Writing is more than an English department priority; it is more than a tool for testing students in whether they know what we think they should. It is a means of readying students for full partnership in the intellectual and social responsibilities of the adult community. Affecting as it does both learning and group interaction, writing is intimately connected, both as process and product, within the educational system and beyond.

Notes

1.   *The Composing Processes of Twelfth Graders* (Urbana, Illinois: NCTE, 1971), p. 97. In "A Writer's Awareness of Audience," Carol Berkenkotter also concludes with a brief discussion of how school writing interferes with the development of rhetorical sophistication by keeping students "topic bound." *College Composition and Communication* 32 (December 1981), pp. 388–399.

2.   Nancy Sommers, "Responding to Student Writing," *College Composition and Communication* 33 (May 1982), pp. 148–156.

3.   Thom Hawkins, *Group Inquiry Techniques for Teaching Writing* (Urbana, Illinois: NCTE, 1976), p.1.

4.   John Dewey, *Experience and Education* (New York: Macmillan, 1963).

5.   For a more complete discussion of the nature of inquiry learning both for individuals and groups, I especially recommend the following: Neil Postman and Charles Weingartner's *Teaching as a Subversive Activity* (New York: Dell, 1969) particularly the chapters on the inquiry method and "languaging" (Chapters 3 and 7); Carl Rogers' *Freedom to Learn* (Columbus, Ohio: Charles Merrill Publishers, 1969); Jerome Bruner's *The Relevance of Education* (New York: W. W. Norton, 1973), for its astute exploration of the function of language in learning; Kenneth Bruffee's "The Brooklyn Plan: Attaining Intellectual Growth Through Peer-Group Tutoring," *Liberal Education* 64 (1978), 447–68 for its pioneering discussion of peer interaction in writing and its carefully sequenced progression of peer response activities; and *Learning in Groups* (see citation below).

6.   Kenneth Bruffee, "Teaching Writing Through Collaboration," in *Learning in Groups,* Clark Bouton and Russell Y. Garth, eds. (San Francisco: Jossey-Bass, 1983), p. 28. See also Bruffee's essay, "Collaborative Learning and the 'Conversation of Mankind,'" *College English* 46 (November 1984), pp. 635–652.

7.   Barry Kroll relates the discovery of purposes and audience among experienced writers to the decentering process of cognitive maturation, noting that more mature writers are able mentally to "construct" the intended audience. ["Cognitive Egocentrism and the Problem of Audience Awareness in Written Discourse," *Research in the Teaching of English* 12 (October 1978), pp. 269–281.]

8.   Alfred Gorman, *Teachers and Learners: The Interactive Process of Education,* 2nd ed. (Boston: Allyn and Bacon, 1974), p. 47.

9.   Shlumo and Yael Sharan, *Small Group Teaching* (New York: Educational Technology Publications, 1976), p.26.

10.   Bruffee, "The Brooklyn Plan," p. 455.

11.   Maxine Hairston's essay, "The Winds of Change: Thomas Kuhn and the Revolution in the Teaching of Writing," [*College Composition and Communication* 33 (February 1982), pp. 76–88] summarizes and evaluates the process paradigm of writing. Janet Emig's seminal essay, "Writing as a Mode of Learning," laid the groundwork of a more inclusive epistemological perspective on writing [*College Composition and Communication* 28 (May 1977), pp. 122–127] while works such as James Moffett's *Active Voice: A Writing Program Across the Curriculum* (Montclair, New Jersey: Boynton/Cook, 1981) emphasize the use of writing not just to test but to teach and generate new knowledge.

12.   In "Writing as Learning Through the Curriculum," Lil Brannon and C. H. Knoblauch explore the limitations of this attitude for fully integrating writing into

the learning process across the disciplines [*College English* 45 (September 1983), pp. 465–474. In a later *College English* essay, Mike Rose shows how the very definition of writing as a "skill or a tool rather than a discipline. . . keeps writing instruction at the periphery of the curriculum." *College English* 47 (April 1985), p. 341. Much the same argument pertains to group interaction.

13.   Clark Bouton and Beryl Rice, "Developing Student Skills and Abilities," in *Learning in Groups* (San Francisco: Jossey-Bass, 1983), p. 32.

14.   Ernest Boyer, *High School: A Report on Secondary Education in America* (New York: Harper & Row, 1983), p. 85.

15.   Art Young, "Considering Values: The Poetic Function of Language," in *Language Connections: Writing and Reading Across the Curriculum,* Toby Fulwiler and Art Young, eds. (Urbana, Illinois: NCTE, 1982), pp. 77–98.

16.   James Kalmbach and William Powers, "Shaping Experience: Narration and Understanding," *Language Connections,* pp. 99–106.

17.   Toby Fulwiler, "The Personal Connection: Journal Writing Across the Curriculum," *Language Connections*, pp. 15–32.

18.   John C. Bean, Dean Brenk, and F. D. Lee, "Microtheme Strategies for Developing Cognitive Skills," *Teaching Writing in All Disciplines,* C. Williams Griffin, ed. (San Francisco: Jossey-Bass, 1982), pp. 27–38.

19.   Stephen Tchudi, *Writing-Across-the-Curriculum: Middle School/Junior High* and *Writing-Across-the-Curriculum: Senior High* (West Haven, Connecticut: NEA Professional Library, 1983).

20.   Neil Postman and Charles Weingartner, *Teaching as a Subversive Activity* (New York: Dell Publishing Co., 1969), Chapter 7.

21.   Marshall Gregory, "A Radical Criticism of the Platonic Foundations of Liberal Education (or, the soul wants what it wants)," *Liberal Education* 69 (Spring 1983), p. 29.

22.   Lewis Thomas, *The Lives of a Cell: Notes of a Biology Watcher.* New York: Bantam Books, p. 16.

2

Conflict and Confusion
Over Sharing Writing

When we picture students working collaboratively on writing, we envision stimulating, thoughtful exchanges among peers, something like our own conferences with students—but better. In removing the potentially intimidating influence of The Teacher, we imagine ourselves unleashing students' pent-up talents and allowing them to blossom in this freer atmosphere. So we carefully teach students to brainstorm ideas, and we prepare questions and devise checklists to guide their revising and editing. Then, expecting anything from minor improvement to miracles, we turn the class over to response groups.

And what do we often find? Students wandering indecisively through each other's drafts, making a comment here, questioning a sentence there, but by and large failing to emulate the purposeful give-and-take that more experienced writers engage in so regularly. Some benefits do crop up—an ambiguous sentence is identified, a grammatical or spelling error is corrected. However, the substantive stuff—exploring purpose, discovering new insights, developing ideas, challenging assumptions—remains unaccomplished.

To bring about our vision of collaborative groups, we need first to see more clearly their actual dynamics, discouraging as they sometimes can be. This chapter and the next two chapters explore peer interaction through information garnered from transcripts, interviews, and observations. The analysis shows how students perceive and carry out the tasks of sharing ideas and reviewing and editing each other's writing. Their interaction suggests five interrelated problems, which I treat as themes, that weave their way throughout the book:

1. confused expectations about the group's purpose and the individual's role in it
2. inability to read group members' texts analytically

17

3. misperceptions about the nature of revision and of writing as a process
4. failure to work collaboratively with group members
5. failure to monitor and maintain group activity.

If we can first understand the nature and causes of these problems, we can more readily anticipate how to structure groups for more effective interaction and more successful writing.

What follows is a segment of a transcript from a sophomore-level composition class composed mostly of juniors and seniors at Michigan State University.[1] The four students in the group had read and commented on each other's papers prior to this session, using a revision guide provided by the instructor and, presumably, modeling their responses on the whole-class revision sessions held throughout the term. Here, they are reviewing each other's essays before preparing a revision to be turned in several days later. The problems these students are having occur among students of all ages; the interaction here is quite typical. Many themes run through this transcript, but I have tried to highlight the most salient ones.

BRENT: Want to do my paper? Really tell me—give me some good criticism on it.

The writer illustrates the assumption common among students that responding to a paper means criticizing it.

It really reeked, I—in my opinion.
CARRIE: I thought it was a good paper—it held my attention.
SHERRIE: Mmm.
BRENT: It's true.
CARRIE: It's like—reading it, you know. I was wondering if something good was going to happen to you, 'cause you kept saying—especially when the coach said *"even* Sweitzer can go out there and make better than a mediocre showing."

Readers immediately deviate from reading the text to inquiring about the story and the person behind it.

BRENT: That *really* happened.
SHERRIE: I would've fallen on my face.
BRENT: Yeah—I kept my cool pretty good. It was a really hard time in my life. But I really didn't—I really didn't say in the paper what I really wanted to say: it wasn't because I was so short so much as because I wasn't a, a schoolboard member's son. . . . I wasn't a schoolboard member's son, I wasn't a teacher's son.

CARRIE: (Her comment is unintelligible.)

BRENT: Yeah—this was a real small town—there was really a lot of hypo-crites, you know.

SHERRIE: How small was it?

BRENT: 16,000.

SHERRIE: The high school was pretty small then.

CARRIE: What I thought you should've done was—in this one, I didn't know if you were um, really confident about going out there, or were you still nervous—you know—when you tried out for the second one—you see what I'm talking about?—when you tried out when you um, were in Michigan. You know.

Group begins to offer advice telling the writer what he should do rather than focusing on their own difficulties in understanding the text as it is.

BRENT: Yeah.

CARRIE: I know you said you aimed to do it in style—but were you still nervous?—were you scared at all, still?

The use of questions helps to probe and clarify meaning, but the group has trouble staying with the question.

BRENT: Yeah (Carrie: Yeah), I could've said that—of course, it was three in the morning (they both laugh)—I really didn't care at that point.

CARRIE: Well, it's all good stuff.

BRENT: As far as grammatical and things like that.

The group shows its ambivalence about being "critical"; they prefer safe, objective commentary.

JIM: It was good. But like I felt that you should have told, added more to the paper, more toward the ending, what happened that senior year, you know, how you felt. I feel I was cut short.

BRENT: (Laughs) Good line!

JIM: 'Cause you know, the coach said you were great—but what happened after that—the rest of the year?

CARRIE: Yeah—it'd be nice to hear the rest of it.

BRENT: You're right—go on with it.

CARRIE: It's just that . . .

BRENT: I didn't think that, though, was directly related to the whole idea of the paper—me being castigated for my height.

CARRIE: Yeah, yeah. Go on with it. I liked this, um, analogy—the ups and downs (little chuckle).

JIM: Yeah.

CARRIE: "The ups and down I was looking for."

BRENT: I originally used the word "indigenous" in there but it sounded too "flowery"—you know, "the ups and downs as indigenous characteristics."

JIM: Wh-where do you come up with these *words*? Are you an English major?

BRENT: No, I used to write a lot 'n; I—I don't know.

SHERRIE: With me, my vocabulary's about this big—I can never think of, you know, a word that . . .

CARRIE: The town in Michigan was bigger?

SHERRIE: Yeah, how big was it?

BRENT: OK, it's Highland, Michigan but—it's smaller, a lot smaller, but it's metro Detroit, which makes it part of the big megalopolis, so it didn't have that kind of down-home attitude. If you were good, you got to play. I did go on and . . .

CARRIE: Very interesting. (They laugh.)

BRENT: How about the, you know—what else d'you have written down there?—"lousy?"

The writer tries to recall the group to the task . . .

CARRIE: Um—no,—I was just going by—let me . . .

BRENT: Transitions and . . .

CARRIE: I like what you said about your goals. I can never set goals. You set one goal early in life—I have never set a goal in my life . . .

SHERRIE: And you went through with it—it was a good paper because of that . . .

CARRIE: If someone would've done that to me, I probably. . . . Something like that would've put me down just far enough that I wouldn't, I wouldn't have the guts to go in and try again—I'd be afraid to be put down again. You deserve a lot of credit for that.

. . . but Carrie's comment pulls them away from the text again and back to the larger context of the story.

BRENT: I was—I was hesitant to take them up on their suggestion because of that—the humiliation of it all (Carrie: Mm-hmm). I was sick to death of it.

SHERRIE: How long?

BRENT: How long?

SHERRIE: Like were you in school?

BRENT: It was my senior year.
SHERRIE: It was your senior year?
BRENT: Yeah.
CARRIE: Yeah—you should put that down.
JIM: And when your coach told you. . .
BRENT: Right—that was my junior year.
JIM: What—that the coach cut you down.
BRENT: Right.
JIM: And then between your junior and senior year you moved?
BRENT: Yeah.
JIM: Who was your paper aimed at?

> *The group recognizes the question of audience for the first time but fails to consider it specifically.*

BRENT: Uh—I'd love to shove it in the face of my coach in Ohio (said very slowly and deliberately). (Chuckles)
CARRIE: Send him a copy! —Um, no—I thought it as aimed at almost anyone.
CARRIE: Really, 'cause anybody could get something out of it.

At this point the group begins to drift aimlessly in their conversation about Brent's experience on the high school basketball team. Their questions and comments on how Brent must have felt have no connection with Brent's draft until Sherrie suggests that readers might need more information. When they periodically return to the draft, they give Brent fragmentary advice on how to fix specific things but never really consider the draft as a whole.

BRENT: Anything else?
CARRIE: When I first started reading that part, "I aimed to do it in style," I didn't know if you made it til the end of the paper—'cause you said, "First a 20-footer." I didn't know if you made the 20-footer or not, you know what I mean?

> *Readers continue to offer vague suggestions but the group fails to develop, test, or apply them.*

BRENT: Oh, yeah, OK.
CARRIE: You know? I thought, "Uh-oh." (Chuckles)
BRENT: I thought it was really vague there too, after I reread it.
CARRIE: You had high hopes.

BRENT: I thought it—you guys might think what I meant by that was "I aimed to do it in style, and first a 20-footer"—like this was my plan. (Chuckles)

Brent show his understanding of the response group as an audience for his work, but they don't know how to respond as readers of an in-process piece of writing.

CARRIE: Yeah, that's—see, that's what I thought.

BRENT: Then I read it again, and I thought, that couldn't possibly be my plan. (They both chuckle briefly.) I don't know—I don't know if that was vague or not—it seemed vague to me.

(Pause)

BRENT: Feel free—feel free to cut me to ribbons—'cause I won't learn anything unless you do.

(Pause)

Brent's implicit definition of criticism as a destructive act is apparently shared by his peers. Despite his invitation, no one really wants to engage in such an unpleasant process.

JIM: What'd you mean by "I never had the opportunity to encounter the kind of ups and downs that I was looking for"?

Jim interprets Brent's request for criticism as an instruction to challenge the writing at the sentence level, primarily to achieve greater clarity. The group still focuses on what the writer intended more than on what the readers experienced.

BRENT: Basketball. It was a direct analogy to basketball.

JIM: Well, I know—I could understand that, but you go, "Curiously enough, the ups and downs that I am alluding to are not the pros and cons of everyday life, but"—I don't know—it seems kind of . . .

BRENT: Redundant, maybe?

JIM: No—

BRENT: ". . . can certainly have its ups and downs. But unfortunately for me, I never"—ah, the first part was just, life in a small town—people can be really rude.

CARRIE: Maybe you should've said something about that—

Carrie's interruption prevents (saves?) Jim and Brent from exploring Jim's question.

'cause I don't think—

BRENT: But that has nothing to do with the paper.

CARRIE : Well, but it—you—it was because it was a small town, wasn't it? That—well, no, because then Highland was a small town too.

BRENT: Yeah.

CARRIE: Yeah, maybe you should've put something about the atmosphere at your school.

Readers appropriate the writer's text by giving vague advice on how to fix the writing rather than asking questions and identifying their own responses.

BRENT: Yeah.

JIM: Why was it that way, or why do you think it was that way?

BRENT: Yeah.

CARRIE: That might take away from the paper too.

BRENT: I want to keep on track, with the height thing.

Brent is not fully willing to entertain his reader's suggestions. His protestations about keeping on track may also be subliminally related to the texture of the discussion as a whole.

CARRIE: Yeah.

BRENT: I didn't want to get off on tangents, that's too easy to do.

SHERRIE: Your senior year.

BRENT: Yeah—I was short and fast.

SHERRIE: Oh, really?

BRENT: So we won games.

JIM: Maybe add on to the end—or just say how you . . . maybe not. Let's see what she says. (A reference to the instructor.)

BRENT: Yeah, I didn't know whether to go on or not. Flip it.

CARRIE: Mmmm.

JIM: That's life. We'd better move on.

The group abandons its task by deferring to a higher authority. They have not been able to reach closure on any of the ideas that arose in discussion, and they dismiss their own authority as readers in deference to the teacher's "right answers."

To Share or Not to Share—The Basic Dilemma

Brent's opening comment represents most students' fundamental ambivalence over exposing their work to peers. "Want to do my paper?" he asks, much as if it will amount to something like an autopsy or the dissecting of a frog. "Really give me some good criticism on it," and later, in a comment that defines what he means by "criticism": "Feel free, feel free to cut me to ribbons." His initial self-deprecation, "It really reeked," serves not only to invite his partners' responses but also to shield himself from potentially cutting criticism by reducing the importance of the paper in his own eyes.

Understandably, writers want help and advice, but they don't want to look foolish. They feel at home with peers but often admit that they doubt their peers' ability to help with revisions. Further, they accept the concept of revision but often remain convinced that *their* drafts are essentially finished. This ambivalence about the task and their peers' role in it is largely justified. Peers' natural reluctance to, as they see it, "criticize" or "evaluate" each other's work along with the rather strong cues they receive from teachers to do just that combine with their own self-doubts about their ability to make responsible judgments regarding others' work. As a result, students in writing groups tend to keep discussion safe, objective, and non-threatening.

As this session on Brent's essay indicates, readers typically begin by reassuring the writer that the piece is basically OK, primarily because the topic was "interesting." Carrie says, "I thought it was a good paper—it held my attention." Later, when the group reviews Jim's paper, Brent begins, "This was a really good paper, I really enjoyed it—kept me on the edge of my seat." In another group, the first reader says, "It's another good story . . . you're really good at description."

Though readers recognize the value of balancing praise with criticism, they implicitly set up a false either-or dilemma. They construe feedback as either positive or negative, praise or blame. With feedback so defined, they choose the safer option of keeping the discussion primarily non-critical. In fact, members of one very successful brainstorming group insisted to me that when it came to reviewing texts, discussing the ideas as they were presented in the paper was simply not an appropriate task—either for students or, implicitly, for teachers.[2] "A paper," explained one member, "has to stand on its own and you shouldn't have to defend or explain it. Besides," she added, "I don't know enough to *evaluate* other people's work." The dichotomy students create effectively rules out much of what we put them in groups to do. Critical generalities and social niceties supplant analysis and even description, since these activities seem to involve "picking things apart." Once you have excluded description, analysis, criticism, and evaluation, there's not much left to do in talking about a text.

Even when writers recognize substantial shortcomings in their own work and ask for help, groups tend to avoid the request, usually by simply ignoring it. In another group, such a request for help, vaguely phrased as it is, serves to end the group's discussion of the writer's paper:

> I don't know, it's kinda hard that part. I mean especially at this paragraph. 'Cause it's such a shapeless . . . it's so hard to explain exactly

what it is, you know. The words . . . I just didn't know what to do, I really didn't.

Carol says, "Um," Carl sidesteps the question by calling for further comments, and they move on to review another student's paper. Linda's helplessness here recalls Brent's unresolved questions at the end of his group's review when he says, "Flip it," and decides to wait for the teacher's more authoritative commentary on his final revision.

Responses like these teach students that their peers have little of real worth to offer, causing the group as a whole to turn to safer, simpler tasks. What should also be clear, however, is that writers seem unable to ask questions in concrete ways and are therefore unable to help the group focus on their concerns. Meanwhile, readers lack knowledge of how to answer questions and, more importantly, how to use the group to find the answer. These matters will be considered in later chapters.

The Preservation of Harmony

Writers' apologies and readers' reassurances stem from a need to preserve harmony within the group. According to the self-reports of a group of freshman writers whom I observed and interviewed over a year's time, the need to establish and maintain harmony (and thus to avoid any vestige of conflict) became the group's primary goal, although it was never expressed as such. Consequently, they avoided focusing on potentially problematic issues; not until much later did they recognize their avoidance strategies. During group meetings, members maintained the paradox of appearing to respond while ducking the real issues. They affirmed writers as individuals while neatly avoiding the words and sentences that comprised their texts.

Thus, their presupposition about the task, combined with their limited interaction skills and their need to preserve harmony within the group, put them in direct conflict with the teacher's expectations that they should help each other think through and rethink their drafts. Students don't initially accept or perhaps understand writing as this kind of process. They have almost always experienced texts as completed rather than emerging products. So, no matter how dissatisfied they may be with their work, it is essentially finished when they come to a response group. Instead students perceive their task as mostly minor tinkering. Groups face the doublesided problem of quelling disharmony among themselves and resisting the intrusions of a teacher whose expectations vary so dramatically from their own.

The Sanctity of Opinions

The reasons behind students' resistance to participating in the process of writing are too varied, complex, and interconnected to wholly account for. But one reason became abundantly clear in Lawson, Holt, and Newell's study that explored freshman attitudes toward questions of personal value and academic standards of evaluation. Interview data revealed that a majority of freshmen believed that challenging, questioning, and especially evaluating students' opinions and beliefs, particularly once they are solidified in writing, is inappropriate both for teachers and students. One student's comment is representative:

> When they send back comments, a lot of papers are based on values and stuff that are a lot of your own opinions, and I have a hard time seeing how they could grade some of your own opinions. Writing style, maybe, technique, or mispelled words, maybe, they could grade on that, but for instance I got a paper back about a week ago. I got a C+ on it and I don't think there were any mispelled words and I doubt there were any sentence problems or paragraph problems, but for some reason he or she [the professor] just didn't match with my ideas.[3]

Facts, they felt, are subject to error and correction because there are right and wrong answers, but since "values and stuff" are personal matters, evaluating them (and all this implies) is merely a reflection of subjective bias and has no place in peer reviews of writing, a preconception for many students that puts them considerably at odds with their teachers' views of writing and peer review.

Thus, the logic of their behavior in groups is consistent with the suppositions about writing that is in any way connected with opinion. This attitude casts a very wide net indeed because, as William Perry found in his research on undergraduates' cognitive development, the ability to distinguish valid from invalid opinions, good ones from bad, seems to develop rather slowly.[4] In the meantime, students' emotional needs on the one hand and linguistic and cognitive abilities on the other are pitted against teachers' expectations and assumptions about the outcomes of group work.

A Comprehensive Framework for Understanding and Developing Group Behavior

Developing successful peer response groups depends on understanding the causes of students' behavior before we can influence the behavior itself. Research into the composing process has begun to do that for writing. Much the same approach needs to be taken to diagnose group behavior. The two have much in common.

Both writing and peer interaction are improved when learners achieve insight into their behavior—its origins, consequences, and relationships with other experiences. The transcript just presented shows that the group has almost no understanding of why they are having the problems they are—either in writing or sharing that writing. In fact, the group seems blissfully unaware of any problems at all. On the other hand, when writers—or groups—are able to perceive strengths and weaknesses in their interaction, as well as the reasons for them, their experience changes from a loose collection of unrelated phenomena to a thematically coherent web in which events are meaningfully connected.

In writing, we call this web *coherence* and seek to teach it by teaching such formal conventions as thesis statements, topic sentences, transitions, introductions and conclusions, and such rhetorical necessities as audience and purpose. In groups, the same web is defined by differentiating what are called *task functions* from *maintenance functions*—the group task as distinct from how the group goes about achieving it—and group members must learn to attend to the maintenance level of their interaction because it weaves together and gives meaning and purpose to the task.

Task functions ride on maintenance functions like telephone conversations on telephone wires: destroy the wire and you destroy the message. The same can be said about writing when it exists as a string of facts, ideas, or observations but lacks the thematic or purposive strand that organizes and holds together all the elements. Like writing, group interaction suffers when members fail to realize the complexity of the medium, becoming absorbed solely in the group task or content.

Group tasks have to do with the groups' immediate need: in peer response groups, sharing and responding to each other's ideas and drafts. Specifically, this involves defining problems, understanding intentions, expressing reactions, proposing alternatives, seeking clarification, asking questions. Underlying these issues, however, and directly influencing them, is the group's self-awareness in carrying out tasks. The ability to step back from the immediate problem to examine group procedures, note evasions or abrupt changes of subject, encourage participation, express feelings, integrate various points of view, summarize, devise alternative approaches—these are the ways in which a group fulfills its tasks. When groups bog down, it is frequently because members assume they have exhausted the task when it's more likely that they haven't developed a strategy for dealing with it. The same might be said about impasses in writing.

Freud's classic analogy of the iceberg is useful here in clarifying this business about functions. Maintenance functions, mostly invisible, provide a foundation for the more visible tasks. How the group goes about its tasks, the group's processes, occupies a larger mass than the tasks themselves, or the group's product. Much the same relationship between product and process in groups carries over to the relationship between content, or ideas, and how they are generated in writing. Exploring the relationships among ideas is probably the most significant source of content available to writers. For example, common to many current techniques of invention (brainstorming, free association, clustering, tagmemics) is a process of recombining old information to produce new ideas. A predominant concern in groups with either task or content leads to overemphasis on outcomes at the expense of the processes that make the outcomes possible.

The issue isn't solely that mature group interaction causes better writing, although in the long run it does, but that in the larger context of writing as a vehicle for learning and thinking, group interaction complements writing by stimulating thinking. If we are concerned with improving written products by improving the processes that generate them, then developing students' interaction skills along with other composing skills comes down to realizing more fully all the implications of writing as a thinking and learning process.

Notes

1.   I am indebted to Professor Mary Francine Danis of Our Lady of the Lake College, San Antonio, Texas for sharing this and other transcripts with me. They were collected for her doctoral dissertation at Michigan State University, "Peer Response Groups in a College Writing Workshop: Students' Suggestions for Revising Compositions," *DAI* 41 (1981).

To ensure as objective an analysis as possible, I've relied heavily on transcripts of students with whom I'm unacquainted. Throughout the book, I supplement my analysis of these transcripts with my own observations of peer response groups drawn principally from visits to discussion groups of the hundred students who participated in the Utah Plan, described in note #2 below. I visited these groups weekly for one term, then monthly throughout the rest of the school year. I followed one group (which is described in Chapter 4) with particular attention; in addition to observing this group, I interviewed the group as a whole twice and individual members frequently. Groups in my own writing classes have also been an important source of instruction.

2.   The group participated in a two-year experimental liberal education program at the University of Utah. A study of this program provided valuable insights into the development of freshman attitudes toward their college experiences, cognitive styles, and values [Jane M. Lawson, Ladd A. Holt, and L. Jackson Newell, "The Utah Plan: College Freshmen in an Experimental Liberal Studies Program" *Journal of General Education* 35 (1983), pp. 136–153.]

3.   Reported in "The Utah Plan: College Freshmen in an Experimental Liberal Studies Program," p. 17.

4.   William Perry, *Forms of Intellectual and Ethical Development in the College Years: A Scheme* (New York: Holt, Rinehart and Winston, 1968), Chapter 5.

3

Reading Peers' Drafts

How do students read each other's drafts? To share writing productively, students need to be able to read another student's work insightfully. This doesn't happen automatically. In fact, much of the reading students do in school teaches them to read very differently. Outside writing classes, teachers ask students to read almost entirely for informational purposes. Research consistently shows that throughout the grades and much of college, students are evaluated principally according to the information they retain.[1] But reading in response groups calls for much more. The group setting confronts students with a raw, unfinished work. Readers need to understand such writing as it is and to anticipate where it might be going before they can help the writer move it toward completion. For both reader and writer, this situation requires considerable tentativeness, open-endedness, and exploration. In a very real sense, reading peer drafts is a collaborative process of construction—of *making* meaning in a text rather than *receiving* meaning from it.

This type of reading goes beyond merely decoding words and understanding facts and ideas; it probably calls for a different order of skills than those associated with (though rarely used in) "critical" reading, such as understanding point of view, determining bias, identifying assumptions, evaluating evidence, sorting facts from opinions and inferences. Reading in response groups demands an active engagement of reader and text in which the reader must sort out not just how well the text works in satisfying the conventions of the particular genre, but also how the text works on the reader in arousing interest, piquing curiosity, conveying ideas, evoking confusion, boredom, or any of an array of possible responses to a text. Readers then must express these reactions as understandable feedback to the writer.

My aim in this chapter is to explore how students read each other's work in a group situation. The analysis of reading presented here serves as a backdrop for the developmental approaches to helping students read peer

29

writing productively, which are presented in Chapter 8. By concentrating here on the problems students experience in reading their peers' work, I hope first to make a case for the continuing process of reading instruction throughout the school years, and second to suggest that peer writing offers perhaps the best opportunity for students to develop the higher order reading skills that we so continually complain they lack. If students flounder at first in reading each other's work, it's not because they are poor readers by nature, but that the task is so big, so new, and yet so important.

Implications of Contemporary Reading Theory

Research in reading over the last fifteen or twenty years has consistently affirmed that reading has perhaps more to do with the reader than with the writer. That is, readers lean heavily on syntactic and contextual cues to predict what a text will mean, and they use the printed words essentially to confirm or modify their initial hypotheses. Kenneth Goodman's research shows that even reading "errors" are more accurately termed "miscues" because they result from misreadings of contexts more than from mistakes in decoding texts.[2] While there is still some disparity between laboratory research techniques and the messier realities of day-to-day reading, little room for doubt remains about the origins of meaning in reading. In *Constructing Texts*, George Dillon concludes "sentences are usually not processed outside of a discourse except in English classrooms and psycholinguistic laboratories. Normally, the discourse context gives top-down guidance in the perception of sentences; it enables readers to project expectations about where the sentence is going and to look for words and phrases that refer to things under discussion and are likely to be coming next."[3] As to where meaning comes from, Dillon concludes that readers construct meaning "by assimilating the text into their body of knowledge and conviction. Otherwise they have acquired but a bunch of meaningless information" (p. 163).

Of course, descriptions of the reading process such as Dillon's probably tell us more about ideal readers than about real ones—at least the readers we find in our classrooms. Essays like Frank Smith's "Twelve Easy Ways to Make Learning to Read Difficult" hint that in "learning to read," students have internalized many of the failings of reading instruction. Smith's "rules" for complicating reading instruction come closer to describing why students demonstrate shortcomings in reading. These four rules are especially suggestive:

1. Teach letters or words one at a time, making sure each new letter or word is learned before moving on.
2. Make word-perfect reading the prime objective.
3. Discourage guessing—be sure children read carefully.
4. Insist upon accuracy.

Students' Reading Processes: Professional Texts

To obtain a fuller picture of how students read school texts, I regularly ask them to free write on how they go about reading particular assignments. In one set of reports on George Orwell's essay, "Politics and the English Language" (a standard selection in college anthologies), 15 of 18 freshmen reported reading in settings inimical to understanding. They read while baby-sitting, waiting in doctors' offices, lounging in the sorority livingroom, watching television, lying in bed before going to sleep, or socializing at home in the family room. All fifteen said that when they came to words or sentences they couldn't understand, they lost the sense of the whole essay. In other words, confronted by a difficult text, they resorted to the *least* effective reading strategies: reading word-by-word or sentence-by-sentence rather than going outside the text to make connections with their own experience or knowledge. This was surprising since the essay culminated a month's reading and writing on the nature of language, especially its relation to thinking, which is mainly what Orwell was talking about. Finally, all these readers tended to equate reading with entertainment; an assignment was "good" if it was "fun" to read. This assumption may account for their choice of reading environments—places associated with leisure reading. And when the text failed to entertain or casually inform, as a newspaper or magazine might, these students assumed its meaning was inaccessible.

The three better readers in the group described a reading experience closer to what we would expect to be "normal." They engaged in pre-reading by looking over the blurb that introduced the essay and reflecting on what they already knew about Orwell. As they read, they made connections between ideas in the essay and what they already knew, and they used these connections not just to affirm some general ideas, but to identify distinctive features of Orwell's approach. The following freewrite shows one student's active engagement with the text, reflecting a vigorous process of making meaning.

Orwell essay! I hope its good. I sure liked his book *A Clergyman's Daughter*. The first couple of paragraphs were deep but I know what he's saying. Our language is becoming too mechanized. I think I understand it in a better way because of that essay we read of Hall's. But to use one of Hall's examples in a different way in relation to Orwell: The brain today has the tendency to be like a computer and all we have to do is enter the subject and all the data, facts, cliches and jargon stored up will come up for us to manipulate. If we are to do what Orwell believes, we must throw away our computer and picture our ideas in our minds through sense and visual pictures. Then through our mental understanding, we can describe our subject—how we feel—but not in computer language. Does this make sense? It does to me. Orwell wasn't hard to understand he was just on another level from what we were used to reading. He's on a high level of thinking that's original rather than a high level of thinking that is mechanized jargon. Our English can come back but it will take clear thinking and clear writing to do this, and in this messed up mechanized world today I don't think it's likely. Since Orwell's time it's only become worse and I don't think we're on the road to recovery now, but rather still on the road to mechanization. The human is becoming the computer: "And man created robot in his own image"

Like the other two strong readers in the group, this student knows about his own reading process; he is aware of what and how he thinks about the text. Compare this response with the more typical one below:

I felt that the essay was kind of hard to understand. It seemed to run on sentences I could kind of grasp what he was saying, but he used a lot of words that were hard to understand. It helped that he gave examples of what the words he was using meant. He used everyday examples that we all can relate to. I believe that there are a lot of politics in our language but I also believe that it should change.

Like most of her peers, this student fails to draw on what she already knows about the subject to find a way into the essay. Her concern with individual words and syntactic structures prevents her from scanning the text to find familiar ideas or concepts; the difficulty of the parts apparently even obscures such rhetorical features as thesis statements and topic sentences which, once identified, would have helped her discover some key ideas. Despite the difficulty this essay presented, all but three of the students in the class naively regarded themselves as average or better-than-average readers.

More descriptive research needs to be done into the dynamics of how students read and process school texts. However, if these findings are generally accurate, they reflect some serious problems. Moreover, if students have this much trouble reading polished professional texts, presumably appropriate to their grade level, what happens when they read unfinished peer writing?

Students' Reading Processes: Student Texts

For some years I have been asking elementary, secondary, and college teachers to reflect on their own presuppositions about student writing by asking them to write responses comparing their reading of a student text with that of a professional text. My purpose has been to reveal to teachers the fault-finding mindset that tends to govern their approach to student writing.

I've begun to include students in the same experiment, asking them to read a piece of expository student writing side by side with a professional expository text and to describe how they read each one. Surprisingly, their reports parallel those of their teachers.

Both sets of readers have a strong predisposition to view the professional writing as good, so they focus primarily on the message and structure of the text. One student writes that she never thought about the topic before in just that way. The language in these protocols is essentially neutral and descriptive; readers identify features in the text that lead them to specific reactions. For example, "the second text uses a short anecdote to begin his essay and uses example as a means to spark interest to the reader." Readers also concern themselves with the writer's possible intentions, using language that is tentative rather than absolute. Overall, readers of professional texts concentrate on what the text says and their own interest or enjoyment in reading it. If ideas are unclear or language is occasionally difficult, they tend to locate the problem in their own shortcomings as readers, not in a failing of the text.

Very different responses emerge from reading a text known to be a student production—as students do in a response group situation. Readers expect such a text to be flawed. The language in the protocols is often negative. Interestingly, rather than adhering closely to the instruction to write about how *they* read the text, most readers begin to catalogue the faults *in* the text. Here, the problems are in the text, not in the reader. Thus, readers show little or no tendency to become engaged in the content. They look *at* the text, not into it, apparently assuming that the writing has nothing very worthwhile to say. For student readers as well as their teachers, professional writing is seen as a legitimate if sometimes inscrutable form of expression; student writing is an exercise, principally a demonstration of "writing problems."

So far, I have been exploring students' reading as it occurs independently. I've suggested that student texts pose some unique problems which are amplified by weaknesses in students' everyday reading strategies—at least of student materials. Low expectations that a student text has much to communicate combine with an "exercise mentality" that drains meaning and purpose from the process of reading and responding to a peer's writing. In his essay "The Language Arts and the Learner's Mind," Frank Smith suggests some reasons why reading and writing can fail to engage students' energies:

> . . . children do not want to learn "speaking," "listening," "reading,"
> and "writing" as isolated skills or as abstract systems; they want to
> understand the world in a far more general sense and to achieve their
> own ends in a far more general sense, and the learning of language in
> any of its external aspects is merely coincidental. Language only be-
> comes complicated and difficult to learn when it is separated from
> other, more general, nonlanguage events and activities in the world. . . .
> There is only one essential precondition for children to learn about

language and that is that it should make sense to them, both in its content and in its motivation.[5]

What we see in these investigations of students' reading, both of professional and student texts, is the legacy of language arts programs in which reading and writing have been treated as empty exercises, designed to meet the school's purposes rather than the student's best interests. Sharing writing in such an environment simply extends the emptiness to the other two language arts, talking and listening. Consequently, in writing groups, students understandably choose to preserve the vitality of their relationships with each other rather than risk their ties with peers over a mere exercise. Despite their private tendency to view student writing as a flawed illustration of "real" writing, students go to great lengths to affirm each other in the face-to-face encounters of a response group. Thus, the group medium itself can exert a powerful influence over how students read each other's texts.

Interpersonal Affirmation in Response Groups

As the transcript in Chapter 2 showed, the text can easily get lost in a response group. Readers tend to affirm the writer-as-person rather than the text-as-embodiment-of-ideas. Carrie's comment to Brent is typical:

> Something like that would've put me down just far enough that I wouldn't, I wouldn't have the guts to go in and try again . . . you deserve a lot of credit for that.

Carrie validates Brent's experience by separating it from the text and by empathizing with the experience and the person. Personal experience narratives especially result in this kind of reading because they enable students to respond to the person rather than the text, all the while believing they are actually reading critically. Sherrie's comment to Brent is particularly telling: "And you went through with it—it was a good paper because of that."

She blurs what she perceives as the goodness of Brent's action into a judgment about the essay itself so that it becomes indistinguishable from her response to his behavior. This approach implies that narrative writing is "good" when readers share the experience on which the writing is based by projecting their own backgrounds or values into the content.

In a study of "Direction and Misdirection in Peer Response," Thomas Newkirk aptly identifies in peer reading a tendency to collapse the subject of the text into the strategies the writer uses in exploring the subject, thus granting the text more transparency than it has. "They were not looking at the window," Newkirk explains, "but the view the window allows them." [6]

Newkirk, too, finds a powerful tendency among student readers to identify with their peers through the texts they produce, an identification strong enough for readers to supply the richness and complexity often missing in the text itself. Newkirk's research suggests, quite usefully, that such readings may signal the distance between the norms of academic readers and those of students. Rather than simply revealing poor readings, Newkirk discovered, students' readings "arise from reasonable assumptions about writing. I was no longer confronted with misreadings, but with different, equally logical readings" (p. 311).

Newkirk suggests that student writers need to master the norms of a new and different community—that of academic readers. It may be, too, that as writers themselves, these readers are still primarily expressive writers, whose chief concern, to quote James Britton, is "explaining the matter to oneself." Their incomplete understanding of the transactional features of writing combines with the need to maintain close, personal ties with each other. Thus students hold their peers' work up against their own standards for expressive prose and simply do not demand the logical and conceptual transformations that expressive writing must undergo to become transactional. Instead, groups can be more concerned with sharing a common experience, unencumbered by a text.

Even with more analytic papers, reading and discussing peer texts can become a process of mutual affirmation conveyed by the personal association the paper evokes. In reading Carrie's paper, Jim remarks,

> I liked—the part I liked the best was the ending—'cause it makes you th—at least ask a question—it makes a person think of what, you know, when is the last time you thought about your country or what the good things are.

Sherrie then makes an association that is another step removed from the paper itself, reflecting that when you travel abroad "you find out how advanced our country is, and how much we do have." Responses like these give the illusion of engagement with texts but really function to strengthen the relationship of the writer with the group of readers.

Reading theorist Louise Rosenblatt distinguishes a continuum between two types of reading: aesthetic reading, which involves participating in and directly experiencing a text, and efferential reading, which readers engage in to carry away a message of some utility beyond the reading situation. The type of reading I'm describing here suggests another kind of experience altogether, one that may not even qualify by these definitions as reading. As Rosenblatt puts it, "perusal of a text merely leading to free fantasy may not be reading at all in the transactional sense [which] . . . emphasizes the relationship with *and continuing awareness of*, the text." [7] For students reading each other's texts, the real value of the experience lies in the texts' potential not directly to delight or instruct, but in the opportunities they offer for revealing and shoring up interpersonal similarities. These similarities serve to promote a safe group environment.

For instance, the review of Brent's paper is largely a request for more background information to the story of his triumph in basketball. His peers are less interested in whether the information is needed to develop the text than they are in finding out more about Brent. Their requests resemble those of young children who ask their parents to embellish a story to make it more entertaining. Though genuinely motivated to help with their peers' writing, students often reveal a strong element of voyeurism as they read each other's work. They "peep" at it not so much to carry something away, as Rosenblatt puts it, as to achieve the gratification of discovering something interesting or unexpected about their fellow students. Moreover, as another group told me, readers need primarily to know how their peers' writing compares with their own, a need which likewise compels them to peep at what their peers have done.

Appropriating the Text

These interpersonal dimensions of the writing workshop—helping a peer, maintaining self-esteem, and sustaining group harmony—can result in egocentric, associative readings of student texts. Egocentricity further influences the reading process because, having used the writing to establish ties among group members, readers then feel free to appropriate each other's texts. Although they offer advice on what needs to be revised, they often seem to be responding to the texts they have in their heads, seemingly unaware that these texts may have little in common with the one the writer wants to develop. Twice, for instance, during the review of Brent's paper, he protests that the group's suggestions are inconsistent with his own. Rather than explore the differences, however, another group member simply changes the subject. No one has (or takes) the opportunity to clarify his or her assumptions and expectations; indeed, the students seem unaware that these differences are significant. They seem too insecure to discuss them comfortably or to articulate them in effective language. Thus they fail to achieve consensus when perspectives contrast, and they also miss the fact that members are responding to very different texts or offering very different ideas about how to improve them.

Another group of writers, freshmen, illustrates the extreme problems that result when, in their egocentric readings of each other's work, students appropriate each other's texts. This group tried to help one member revise his draft by having each member make suggestions on how to change it. They reported, with considerable frustration, that after the revision session the writer was so confused he just gave up on the whole topic and started something new, in essence defeating the task by submitting one draft to the group and an equally fresh draft to the teacher, this one uncomplicated by peer input.

By appropriating their peers' texts, response groups can create the illusion of productivity while actually skirting the task of sharing ideas and collaborating on revision. As a result, students in revision workshops often write in isolation, viewing their own drafts as essentially finished products rather than recognizing—or, more probably, knowing how to fulfill—their roles as collaborators on works-in-process.

New Directions for Reading and Discussing Student Texts

Throughout this examination of reading strategies in response groups, two elements have been largely absent: *consciousness of process* and *meaningful dialogue.* The former involves the ability to distinguish content from process, the *what* from the *how.* As I suggested earlier, this is fundamental to successful group interaction. Here we see the same problem through another window: consciousness of process is equally essential to reading and discussions. Ann Berthoff calls it "consciousness of *consciousness,*" or "minding the mind," and proposes that "consciousness in meaning-making activity always involves us in interpreting our interpretations; thinking is a matter of 'arranging our techniques of arranging'; criticism is a matter of coming to 'know our knowledge.' . . . The point is that we can learn to take advantage of that fact, making the raising of consciousness about the making of meaning our chief strategy in teaching the circularity of all knowledge and in developing a 'pedagogy of knowing.' "[8] As I argue in subsequent chapters, such a "pedagogy of knowing" is accessible through collaborative sharing of writing because it gets students outside themselves.

To make this sharing productive, teachers must find ways to introduce the second element missing from the student interaction examined so far—dialogue. Paulo Freire offers one of the finest definitions of dialogue I know, sexist language notwithstanding. His definition sets a standard toward which peer response groups must aspire:

> Dialogue imposes itself as the way by which men achieve significance as men. Dialogue is thus an existential necessity. And since dialogue is the encounter in which the united reflection and action of the dialoguers are addressed to the world which is to be transformed and humanized, this dialogue cannot be reduced to the act of one person's "depositing" ideas in another, nor can it be a simple exchange of ideas to be "consumed" by the discussants.[9]

Transforming and humanizing the world may be beyond the reach of a peer response group, but the notion of collaborative sharing of reflection and action is absolutely central. As I will show in subsequent chapters, full partnership in the sharing of writing cannot begin until everyone involved engages in dialogue as Freire describes it here. For the revision of drafts, the action component—actively rethinking and rewriting, not just talking about it—is especially necessary, and just as much overlooked.

Notes

1.   See Arthur Applebee, *Teaching English in the Secondary Schools* (Urbana: NCTE, 1981) and D. Trachtenberg, "Student Tasks in Text Materials: What Cognitive Skills Do They Tap?" *Peabody Journal of Education* 52 (1974), pp. 54–57.
2.   Kenneth Goodman, "Reading: A Psycholinguistic Guessing Game," *Journal of the Reading Specialist* 4 (May 1967), pp. 126–135.
3.   George Dillon, *Constructing Tests: Elements of a Theory of Composition and Style* (Bloomington: Indiana University Press, 1981), p. 6.
4.   Frank Smith, "Twelve Easy Ways to Make Learning to Read Difficult," *Essays into Literacy* (London: Heinemann Educational Books, 1983), p. 11, rpt. from Frank Smith (Ed.) *Psycholinguistics and Reading* (New York: Holt, Rinehart and Winston, 1973).
5.   Frank Smith, "The Language Arts and the Learner's Mind," in *Essays into Literacy*, p. 71.
6.   Thomas Newkirk, "Direction and Misdirection in Peer Response," *College Composition and Communication* 35 (October 1984), p. 308.
7.   Louise Rosenblatt, *The Reader, the Text, the Poem: The Transactional Theory of the Literary Work* (Carbondale, Illinois: Southern Illinois University Press, 1978), p. 29.
8.   Ann E. Berthoff, *The Making of Meaning,* (Montclair, New Jersey: Boynton/ Cook, 1981), p. 44.
9.   Paulo Freire, *Pedagogy of the Oppressed* (New York: Continuum Press, 1982), p. 77.

4

Revising in Groups—
Reconceiving or Rewording?

Two mutually reinforcing assumptions affect revision in response groups. First, while students recognize that response groups are helpful to the writing, they also believe groups are bound to be unpleasant for the writer. Students' immediate need for harmonious personal relations conflicts with their more distant need to improve their writing. Second, students lack both an understanding of and experience with revising their work. They are initially skeptical that describing, analyzing, testing, modifying, or challenging each other's ideas can really help, bound up as these activities are in the ominous concepts of "criticism" and "evaluation."

These assumptions divert students' attention from the writing to the writer. Thus, they limit possibilities for sharing and revising ideas that reside in their drafts. Groups flounder when students restrict themselves to tinkering with details rather than fully accepting the tasks of inventing and revising, which involve the more active processes of conceptualizing and restructuring. This chapter explores the origins and limitations of group revision strategies.

Lexical vs. Conceptual Revision

A growing body of research is documenting the limited revision strategies of inexperienced writers. Nancy Sommers' reknowned 1980 study of freshman revisions noted that the term *revision,* although familiar to students, didn't describe their view of what they were actually doing in rewriting. Instead, Sommers found, these students viewed their task as a "rewording activity"—a process of lexical substitution and mechanical clean-up. For experienced adult writers, on the other hand, revision is central to the process of "discovering meaning," so as they revise they are aware that they are "finding the form or shape of their argument."[1]

39

In a study of twelfth grade writers, Lillian Bridwell also found that lexical and surface level revisions were most frequent. More important, however, is her finding that papers with the lowest quality ratings were "revised" most extensively because, as she observes, "these students hardly re-read their papers before they began again with a new version."[2] Bridwell's finding parallels the experience of the student in the preceding chapter who submitted one draft to his response group and a "revision" to his teacher that was really an entirely different paper. In contrast, writers of highly rated papers in Bridwell's study concentrated on reworking the language of existing sentences rather than giving up on one approach to try a new one.

Sommers' and Bridwell's findings offer disturbing contrasts. Experienced writers in Sommers' study succeeded by altering whole chunks of discourse as they explored new meanings, while students in Bridwell's study wrote the poorest papers when they tried precisely the same procedures. This contrast may suggest that many student writers are not developmentally ready to assume more holistic perspectives on their own and their peers' work. Complicating matters further is Donnalee Rubin's study in which she argues that the critical reading abilities of freshmen, including their ability to diagnose writing problems, develop more rapidly than their ability to transfer and apply this knowledge to solving their own writing problems. In other words, they can read each other writer's work for concepts, themes, and arguments, and they understand intellectually the meanings of criteria such as focus, coherence, and support. But they continue to write and revise their own texts at the surface and lexical levels.[3]

In groups, students deal with texts, their own and each other's, in the same ways these studies describe independent revision. Although readers ask a few general questions to establish the group milieu, the bulk of their discussion initially centers on rather formalistic concerns over clarity, questions devoted especially to word choice, grammar, and mechanics. Some groups become almost completely concerned with such matters. Consider these exchanges from the discussion of Carrie's paper:

BRENT: This is a really good transition, here in the beginning—you say, "Then last summer I took a trip to Ireland." Interesting . . . you know how to spell "thoroughly"? . . . You have 'throughly'."

(Carrie: little laugh)

BRENT: "Negative" is spelled with an "a," not an "i."
CARRIE: I have so many typographical errors—I didn't . . .
BRENT: Um—did you mean "ample," like (unintelligible)?
CARRIE: No—it was "amount"—I hit the "p" instead of the "o."
BRENT: Oh—

CARRIE: My finger hit the wrong—
BRENT: "The amount of babies"—
CARRIE: It still amazes me, the amount of babies . . .
BRENT: Amount—is "amount" the right word to use when you're speaking of human beings? You make it sound like a pile of trash—or a pile of garbage—maybe "number."
CARRIE: "the number of babies"
SHERRIE: Yeah.

And another group, reading Chuck's paper:

LINDA: I liked the word "gambler" though.
CAROL: Yeah, cause I think that it, you know, you were kind of betting on who could drive better and who could, uh . . .

And later, on Chris' paper:

KATE: I thought there were just some really good words, like "frantic." I thought that was um—"frantically trying to get up—" I think it worked really well.

These exchanges suggest that lexical and mechanical revisions serve to assure the group members that they are really helping each other while, in fact, they avoid the swamplands of "criticism" in favor of the safer terrain of correct, factual answers. However, if Rubin's thesis is correct, then students' attention to lexical and grammatical details in their peers' writing may not be entirely a manifestation of either poor reading ability or cognitive immaturity.

More likely, this behavior reflects a choice, albeit an unconscious one, to focus on surface features at the expense of concepts. The fact that these features leap out from the page, along with most students' expectation that marking them is a teacher's foremost concern, provides a powerful predisposition toward making this choice. But *choice* it is, based as I've suggested on a false dichotomy of praise or blame, positive or negative criticism that rigidly limits the options students believe are available to them. Consequently, what students lack in using their ability to read for concepts and structure is an understanding that their own choices, more than roles imposed on them, influence their behavior.

Revising, Group Process, and Metacognition

Metacognition, however unwieldy the word, has to do with thinking about thinking, or in Berthoff's terms, minding the mind. In groups, metacognition is related to an awareness of how the group functions. In fact, groups can't explore problems of group behavior without reflecting self-consciously on their own actions. Conversely, groups that become stuck approaching a task in a particular way typically fail to think metacognitively and thus lack insight into their "stuckness."

The following discussion shows the need for a group to think about its thinking to get beyond the lexical impasse they have reached. This is one of the few overt disagreements within a group that I've ever seen; it focuses on a single word:

CARL: I don't like the word "enjoy."

LINDA: I think that's the point, though. Up—until she hears that you know, I mean, her dad was gone.

CARL: I don't know, I still don't like that word "enjoyment."

LINDA: I do!

CARL: Maybe uh . . .

LINDA: I think—I think that's exactly it.

CARL: Maybe—just "be able to relax and overlook the excitement," or "view the excitement," or . . . The word "enjoy," it seems like you had a smile on your face and—

LINDA: You feel it's awkward?

CAROL: Well, maybe I should ex-

CARL: Yeah.

CAROL: Um, go into further explanation. It's something that—uh, I *did,* and you know, it was a really neat—You know, the whole. . .

LINDA: I mean you feel like you're in a movie scene or—you know what I mean.

CARL: . . . see that's . . .

CAROL: I know, I—maybe I'm a little bit—sadistic or something.

LINDA: But I know what you mean!

KATE: But I—sirens are—can get my blood going.

CAROL: I just, you know . . . I don't know.

LINDA: I really do. I di—I really did enjoy (laughs).

CARL: I just took a little offensive to the word, uh "enjoy." I just didn't like the way it was used. But it's your writing.

LINDA: But you know, I . . .

CARL: It's up to you.

LINDA: After, you know, Dad died, the you know, enjoyment, or excitement just disappears, bingo like this.

CAROL: Right.

LINDA: In a snap, because you realize what's going on, uh, you know finally—and I think that's emphatic that way.

CARL: Using that word "enjoy"?

LINDA: Yeah, I do!

CARL: When I just read it, when I just stopped afterwards I said, how could she use the word "enjoy," you know, I mean before you even got through all the paper, you know, just—

KATE: Well, did you . . . think that right at the very beginning, there was something—very serious?

CARL: No, no, not at all. I—don—I just don't see, if I see my Dad in pain, that this could be an enjoyable thing, you know what I mean.

CAROL: Oh, I see.

CARL: The whole surroundings.

CAROL: The whole—thing.

CARL: Well it's up—You know, it's just my own feeling on that part.

CAROL: No, I see what you were saying. I don't know, I guess I just never at the . . . at the time, just—you know . . .

KATE: Well being as young as you are, too, are you 14?

CAROL: It was just a—new—you know, I mean, it was exciting—a new, you know—I mean, I see what you're saying, I . . . I . . . I . . .

KATE: Well you didn't know, like—like you said you didn't—it wasn't serious.

CAROL: No. No, I—(heh-heh)

CARL: . . . I don't know. I—I can see your point, too, but it's just when I read it, it just sort of hit me bad.

LINDA: I see.

CARL: Okay, on the bottom of the second page . . .

Carl's disagreement with Carol's term shows the self-defeating consequences of lexical tinkering. More important, however, the discussion illustrates their inability to think and talk about how they are approaching this particular problem. Although the discussion concentrates on a single word, Carl is certainly concerned with more than diction. He seems to be grappling unaware with the larger and more significant conflict of how one can experience enjoyment in circumstances surrounding a parent's death—a far more engaging and stimulating topic than the simple narrative Carol had written. If recognized as such, this hidden topic might have made for more meaningful use of the group's energies and led to a true revision. But no one realizes that their strategy at the task level is taking them nowhere, or how to shift from there to the maintenance level, to say something like, "We seem to be stuck on this word 'enjoy.' That must mean that it's not the word we're arguing about but something bigger—the concepts it stands for. What are we really saying?" Instead, Carl bullies Carol and her defender, Linda, into submission. They both concede, "I see" when they probably don't see at all, apparently just to end the debate. Their failure to "read" the group's behavior parallels their failure to read the draft: both readings are carried out at the surface level, obscuring the underlying structure which is vastly richer and potentially more informative. (See Chapter 7 for a more extensive discussion of the relation of structure to meaning, in both groups and texts.)

Teachers and Miscues

The more consequential feedback about logic, organization, and significance typically comes almost exclusively from teachers, and it is often at odds with peers' assurances. However, teachers' feedback also implicitly tends to affirm the value of lexical revisions, so the subtle messages that students receive from their teachers powerfully shape their expectations about revising—either alone or in groups—regardless of the contradictions with teachers' expressed desires for substantive revision through group interaction.

Despite the general recognition that revision is central to writing and must be given special emphasis in teaching, our theoretical assumptions about the holistic nature of revision are often at odds with classroom practices that reward tinkering with details. At the theoretical level, for instance, Donald Murray conceives revision comprehensively, asserting that "the writer moves from a broad survey of the text to line-by-line editing, all the time developing, cutting, and reordering." [4] Ideally, revision ends in some form of publication, so it necessarily includes editing and proofreading. More central to the *process* of writing, however, is a prior phase of revision, about which Murray maintains that writing is really rewriting since "revising becomes rehearsal as the writer listens to the piece of writing." [5] These two phases of revision correspond roughly with the two types of peer reading I've been describing—tinkering with surface features and rethinking larger issues.

Bridwell's study of revision encompasses both extremes of reading and revising. She identifies seven levels of activity, from the surface level to the multi-sentence and finally the text level, and she concludes that twelfth graders are more successful at revising for lexical and mechanical matters than at rethinking and restructuring. Yet conceptually-based revision, like conceptual reading, are most necessary for inexperienced writers. Clearly, revising is a multi-level activity, nor is it always possible to distinguish one level from another. Generally, though, writers need to devote more of their efforts to rethinking and restructuring their drafts, delaying revisions of words and mechanics until just prior to "publication"—whether this is for peers, a broader public, or simply the teacher. I've argued that students primarily *choose* to ignore the more essential aspects of revision in favor of safer, more objective responses to their peers' work. But it's also true that in classrooms they are often instructed to consider the pieces at the expense of the whole. In the conclusion of her study, Sommers sketches the role teachers play in determining students' revision strategies:

> Inexperienced writers' revision strategies are teacher-based, directed towards a teacher-reader who expects compliance with rules—with

pre-existing "conceptions"—and who will examine only parts of the composition (writing comments about those parts in the margins of essays) and will cite any violation of rules in those parts. At best the students see their writing altogether passively through the eyes of former teachers or their surrogates, the textbooks, and are bound to the rules which they have been taught.[6]

The responses students receive to one piece of writing effectively teach them what will be expected from the next. When students are rewarded for lexical and grammatical competence at the expense of conceptual and organizational sophistication, groups may simply magnify students' legitimate preoccupation with these details. In contrast to the limited resources writers have as individuals, the group provides a larger pool from which to draw, a pool where someone is likely to question a word, correct a misspelling, or supply appropriate punctuation. In this respect, groups are doing what they do best—sharing individual resources to solve problems that the individual couldn't solve alone. Their energies are simply misdirected.

One of James Britton's findings suggests the subtle ways teachers may unintentionally shape students' expectations about and approaches to reading their peers' work: "The small amount of speculative writing certainly suggests that, for whatever reason, curricular aims did not include the fostering of writing that reflects independent thinking; rather, attention was directed towards classificatory writing which reflects information in the form in which both teacher and textbook traditionally look at it."[7] To the extent that writing is assigned and read for its ability to organize and convey information rather than to explore ideas, peer readers may have internalized a reading stance of checking primarily for accuracy of presentation.

The absence of what might be called "speculative reading" parallels the absence of speculative writing, with results similar to those Britton described: inexperience in the challenging, analytical modes of response necessary for students to get beyond the recording of information. Although students regularly make sense of texts more complicated than those of their peers, they read largely to store up facts for the next quiz. Thus they have been trained into reading habits of a lower order than what we expect in groups.

As I suggest in Chapter 7, the teacher's role in setting up group response sessions and whole courses is crucial in altering these habits and expectations. The learning log, for instance, is a place to teach students how writing can be used to raise questions and speculate about ideas. Having students periodically read selections of their log to the class and respond to their peers' questions and observations helps to define their writing as a stimulus for thought rather than a catalog of writing flaws. I usually set aside a class period every two weeks and assign four or five students to read a page or two from their log to the rest of the class and then to be in charge of the discussion that follows.

By assigning the rest of the class to write on the same topic for that day, I find that they are prepared to ask questions, challenge points of view, or contribute their own thoughts. I become just another participant.

The teacher's role in group response sessions also influences how students read and respond to each other's work. In the early stages of a course, I model ways to pull back from the details of a draft by asking writers to make one-sentence statements of purpose and asking readers to make one-sentence descriptions of what main idea they got out of the draft. This is especially useful in working with personal narratives, where inexperienced writers tend to chronicle events without giving much thought to their purpose. Consider the following exchange:

SPEAR: Mitch, can you tell us in one sentence what you're trying to help your readers understand from writing about the events you've just described?

MITCH: One sentence, huh?

SPEAR: Yeah—what do you want us to take away from reading this—not about you personally but about how you learned about nuclear weapons.

MITCH: Well, I think I want them to see that every time I learned something new I thought I knew it all, but there was still a lot I didn't know.

SPEAR: Diane, what do you think you'd take away from reading Mitch's narrative? Can you sum it up in one sentence?

(long pause)

DIANE: Um, I think I'd see how our questions can keep getting better—that we'll always be unsure about some things but we can kind of keep opening up.

MITCH: Yeah, it's really about how hard it is to learn about this.

SPEAR: Good! What I'm trying to show you here is that asking each other questions like these can keep you focused on these bigger issues of what you're trying to achieve in your writing and what your readers are getting out of it. Greg, why don't you try the same thing with your piece and I'll check back later. Thanks.

For at least the first month it's important to keep students' attention focused on such larger concerns and to make them aware of how my questions and responses in their groups help them talk about their writing at this level.

In addition to shaping students' attitudes by way of the writing and reading we put them to, teachers can misguide group discussion in a more direct way, by devising checklists, guidelines, or questions intended to clarify tasks and keep the group on course. Generally, these handouts serve one of two purposes: either for reviewing a paper prior to the group session or for guiding and structuring the discussion. Three such guides are reproduced below. All are problematic.

EXAMPLE 1.

COMPOSITION CHECKLIST
Expository/Analytical
(Secondary School)

Writer's Name _____ Date _____

Title of Composition _____

Writer:

1. Review your composition for each of the following elements.
2. Revise your composition until you feel that it represents your best work.
3. Clip this checklist to your composition and give it to another student to read and evaluate.

CONTENT:

_____ 1. Has clear purpose or point.
_____ 2. Provides a title that suggests what the point is.
_____ 3. Seems to have a specific audience in mind. (Name the person or group.) _____
_____ 4. Gives at least three necessary examples, facts or details to make the point clear.
_____ 5. Arranges ideas in the best order.
_____ 6. Begins each paragraph with a clear topic sentence or idea.
_____ 7. Keeps the discussion in each paragraph centered around the topic idea.
_____ 8. Shows clear relationship among paragraphs.
_____ 9. Uses an opening sentence to catch the attention of the reader.
_____ 10. Emphasizes the purpose or point in a concluding sentence or paragraph.
_____ 11. Uses exact words and complete sentences to help the reader understand the purpose.

CONVENTIONS:

_____ 1. Uses a subject in each sentence that agrees with the predicate verb.
_____ 2. Has a clear antecedent for each pronoun.

_____ 3. Begins each sentence with a capital letter and ends with a suitable mark of punctuation.

_____ 4. Has no misspelled words. (Check in a dictionary all words you are not sure of.)

_____ 5. Employs correct punctuation marks within the sentences.

_____ 6. Uses the standard form for heading, margins, and spacing.

EXAMPLE 2.

RESPONSE GROUP GUIDE
(Secondary English)

1. Know the names of those in your group.
2. One student reads his/her paper out loud first.
3. Group members will, one at a time, point out good points like use of specific details, exact nouns and verbs, good action, good pictures, interesting details, etc.
4. Group members will, one at a time, make suggestions to help the writer add, change, move, delete, clarify, etc.
5. Group, as a whole, will help with mechanics: spelling, punctuation, capitals, complete sentences.
6. Go on to next student in the group.

EXAMPLE 3.

REVISION GUIDE FOR WRITING WORKSHOPS
(Freshman Composition)

Topic and Thesis

1. no clear thesis or argument
2. thesis too broad for the length of the composition
3. thesis not worth arguing

Composition as a Whole

1. Loose or unclear organization
   a. illogical division of subject
   b. incoherence of parts
   c. illogical sequence of ideas or paragraphs
   d. random or circular flow of ideas; repetitiousness
2. unimaginative or routine treatment of subject
3. tendency to belabor the obvious

4. Introduction
   a. over long
   b. over general;
   c. irrelevant
   d. lacking in a provocative "hook" to catch reader's interest
5. Conclusion
   a. anticlimactic
   b. too abrupt
   c. irrelevant or repetitious

Reasoning and Evidence

1. lack of sufficient evidence or illustration; over-reliance on generalizations or unsubstantiated opinion (USE EXAMPLES)
2. inaccurate evidence (Don't distort evidence to "prove" a point)
3. fallacious reasoning
   a. distortion
   b. oversimplification
4. failure to take important opposing arguments into account
5. generally sloppy or superficial thought

Sentence Structure

1. sentence fragments
2. run-on sentences
3. comma errors
4. misplaced or dangling modifiers
5. faulty agreement of subject and verb
6. faulty agreement of noun and pronoun
7. faulty parallelism
8. shift of
   a. subject (in mid-sentence)
   b. verb tense
   c. verb voice (active, passive)
9. ambiguous pronoun reference
10. passive voice or under-reliance on strong, active verbs
11. over-reliance on linking verbs (is, was) or "there is" "it is" constructions
12. inadequate subordination of modifiers to main clause; over-reliance on short simple sentences
13. sentences relatively unvaried in structure and length
14. illogical or clumsy word order
    a. awkward
    b. ambiguous
    c. unemphatic

Paragraph Structure

1. too short and choppy
2. lack of necessary transitions between paragraphs
3. lack of necessary topic sentences to control and direct main idea
4. failure to achieve coherence
   a. lack of transitions within the paragraph
   b. lack of necessary pronouns
   c. lack of repetition of sentence patterns (parallelism) to emphasize relatedness (similarity or contrast of ideas)
5. unclear, unsequential, illogical development of thought

Diction
(Word Choice)

1. imprecise, ambiguous, misleading or poorly chosen words or phrases
2. overly general, vague
3. inappropriate level of usage (overly formal, colloquial, simplistic)
4. stilted or abstruse language or trite language; reliance on clichés
5. bland, not vivid or imagistic; failure to employ such figures of speech as metaphors, similies, analogies where appropriate
6. verbose or redundant

Mechanics and Form

1. spelling
2. proofreading
3. punctuation
4. legibility

These examples share two problems. They interfere with writing as process and they ask students to assume the reading stance of the writing teacher.

How do they obstruct process? Although all three attempt to convey priorities for revision by distinguishing content from conventions, whole from part, the itemized format presupposes that the writing is in a form stable enough to warrant such close analysis as the guides call for. In other words, the guides are product-centered. In pushing students toward point-by-point analysis, they not only obscure the whole text but seal off the processes that could help it continue to evolve. Example 2 is especially limiting. It instructs students to point out specific details—nouns, verbs and images—before it calls for suggestions. Nor does it allow for questions. The guide thus predisposes students to comment exclusively on particulars.

As I've suggested, close analysis of this sort is entirely appropriate toward the end of the composing process. If guides like these were used only for final revision they could serve a useful purpose (although the negative language of

Example 3 tends to turn a peer review into something closer to an inquisition). More often, however, teachers fail to distinguish the type of revision they expect and the appropriate times for each kind. Instead they merge the conceptual aspects of revision with the technical, using guides like these to cover both aspects in a single sitting, apparently expecting students to figure out the correct priorities for themselves.

Such exercises reflect a confusion of process with product. Students are asked to march (or in the third example, race) through the lists making cursory, often exclusively formalistic comparisons of their papers against the guide. They never really get to consider the whole text. Example 1 is particularly misleading in exhorting the student to present his or her "best work" to the group and directing the reader to "evaluate" it. This suggests that the draft should be essentially finished and implies that the writer's role is to expose her ignorance to the group so that they may uncover problems she couldn't find and correct on her own. Consequently, these guides fail to teach students to engage in genuine revising activities; instead they establish very clearly that what counts are results. The guides are entirely task-oriented, providing no opportunity for students to reflect on their work as a group and consider how their interaction contributed to the outcomes of their discussion.

These handouts also skew students' attitudes toward revising by asking them to read each other's texts as teachers do. Ironically, the greatest shortcoming in teachers' readings of students' texts is probably that they find it irresistible to read the text against their own mental checklists of conventions— conventions in form, mechanics, even content. When we do this, we have stopped reading the text for what it communicates about the subject and begun reading for what it says about the writer, especially about his or her shortcomings.

This sort of reading may be inevitable in teachers. And when these mental checklists succeed in accounting for the whole composition as well as its parts, such reading reflects the unique contribution teachers make to the writing class. However, through group guides that direct students to read as teachers do, teachers misdirect students' readings of peer texts. When students "fail" to read in this way, we conclude that they cannot read "critically." When they succeed, as I will show in the next chapter, they adopt an unfortunate and poorly executed role as surrogate teachers within the group. Thus, students are often in a no-win situation.

Extending the Composing Process

Throughout this chapter I've emphasized that the limitations of peer revision stem not just from lack of ability or intellectual readiness to read and revise effectively but from more basic confusions about the nature of process

and product in students and teachers alike. These confusions manifest themselves in a number of ways:

1. miscues from teachers that collapse process into product, obscuring the
   process;
2. students' lack of interaction skills, affecting both their reading and revision of their peers' drafts;
3. restrictive reading strategies.

Fortunately the interdependency of these three problems gives them
something of a domino effect: knocking down one problem tends to topple
the other two. Careful and systematic use of peer discussion seems most
likely to give those dominoes the nudge they need. More than teacher-centered
pedagogies, peer interaction can stimulate the connected processes of writing,
reading, and learning. Groups provide purpose and audience, giving inexperienced writers more reason to revise. Equally important, groups help to prolong the composing process, keeping it alive and leavening writers' egocentricity with the yeasty contributions of other readers.

One of Bridwell's findings is crucial here: "The longer the student had
to explore his or her ideas," she concludes, "the more likely he or she was to
add, delete, or substitute extended segments of discourse." [8] By convening
groups for two or more revision sessions on the same paper and structuring
the activities of each session, teachers can prevent students from prematurely
turning drafts into completed texts. (See Chapter 11 for a sequence of such
guides.) By sequencing group tasks, teachers also allow themselves time
to integrate instruction in the skills associated with rethinking drafts: not
just adding, deleting, or substituting information, but reading, listening, providing feedback, and, concurrently, assessing writing and improving group
interaction.

These skills are necessary to develop writing in its larger context of
thinking and learning. They strike a delicate balance between writing and
writer's block: on one hand the continued generation of ideas and on the
other the many modifications that constitute revision. These modifications
include the ongoing checking of drafts against writers' intentions and readers'
responses, against conventions of logic, style, and expression, and against
peer input—all of which need to guide and nourish revision rather than stop it.

Revision is inevitably bound up with evaluation—both others' evalua-
tions of our work and our own. Writers at all levels of experience evaluate
their writing continuously; it's an element in the process. The goal, however,
is not to let evaluation become a highly charged emotional issue, especially
to the extent that students and teachers alike find themselves evaluating
writers and writing and letting those judgments stand as terminal points in
development. Instead we need to take a neutral stance—to understand evaluation as a normal feature of the gradual development of writing.

When peer interaction is a central feature of the extended writing/learning process, students become more likely to integrate evaluation with revision. When this occurs, evaluation doesn't happen after writing; it becomes part of the group's assessment of what they *are learning*, not what they *have learned.* (Chapter 7 explores this distinction in greater detail.) Brian Johnston's study of the motivational effects of writing assessment points in much the same direction. This Australian survey of over a thousand English teachers indicates that "students whose teachers attempted to lead them toward their own self-assessments reported a higher level of motivation to improve their writing than did students who were experiencing the judgmental approach to assessment [e.g. grades or comments] ."[9]

As the reading and revision behaviors considered in these chapters suggest, self-evaluation applies as much to assessing—or perhaps more accurately "describing"—group behavior as it does to assessing or describing writing. Integrated into the peer review process, self-evaluation can become part of the self-reflective thinking absent in so much of students' oral and written discourse.

Notes

1.   Nancy Sommers, "Revision Strategies of Student Writers and Experienced Adult Writers," *College Composition and Communication* 31 (December 1980), p. 384.

2.   Lillian Bridwell, "Revising Strategies in Twelfth Grade Students' Transactional Writing," *Research in the Teaching of English* 14 (October 1980), p. 216.

3.   Donnalee Rubin, "Evaluating Freshman Writers: What Do Students *Really* Learn?" *College English* 45 (April 1982), pp. 373–379.

4.   Donald M. Murray, "Writing as Process: How Writing Finds Its Own Meaning" in *Eight Approaches to Teaching Composition,* Timothy R. Donovan and Ben W. McClelland, eds. (Urbana, Illinois: NCTE, 1980), p. 5.

5.   Donald M. Murray, "Writing as Process," p. 5, see also *A Writer Teaches Writing* (New York: Houghton Mifflin, 1968), and "Teach the Motivating Force of Revision," *English Journal* 67 (1978), pp. 56–60.

6.   Sommers, p. 383.

7.   James Britton, *The Development of Writing Abilities, 11–18* (London: Macmillan, 1978), p. 197.

8.   Bridwell, p. 210.

9.   Brian Johnston, "Non-Judgmental Responses to Students' Writing," *English Journal* 71 (April 1982), p. 50.

5

Moving from Teacher Surrogate to Peer Collaborator

Exploring group behavior is a little like excavating an archeological site. Schliemann dug through at least seven layers to uncover Troy. Every layer seemed complete in itself but hinted tantalizingly at something more underneath. Similarly, however fully one seems to account for students' behavior in groups, there are always deeper questions about prior causes. I can't explain or even fully understand all the origins of group behavior; eventually speculation replaces interpretation. But one more layer needs to be unearthed because it yields a common cause for many of the anxieties and shortcomings discussed so far—the allure of the teacher surrogate. To initiate group work teachers need to replace students' automatic assumption that they are to become substitute teachers with an understanding of the more useful role of peer collaborator. When this occurs, students are better able to balance content and process in response groups because collaborative relationships include an enhanced responsibility not just for achieving results but for setting goals and monitoring progress as well.

The Teacher Surrogate

Partly because they have no other models of school experience on which to draw, partly because they receive unclear or misleading cues from teachers, writers and readers alike define their roles in response groups along the familiar lines of the teacher/student relationship. As it is played out in groups, this relationship is often anxiety-ridden and somewhat antagonistic; it is based on a stereotype of the teacher as an authority figure who dispenses knowledge and passes judgment on the struggling student. So ingrained is this stereotype that it can block the emergence of genuinely collaborative relationships and the very different modes of interaction these relationships involve.

According to the stereotype, teachers are responsible for orchestrating discussion. Their comments range from advice to dogmatic pronouncements. They are supposed to have answers for all questions. They are omniscient, so they can anticipate questions before they are asked and divine intentions without those intentions being expressed. Their greater knowledge and experience justifies teachers' roles as judge and critic and the students' roles as follower and supplicant. Students tend to assume these stereotyped roles with the writer playing the student and readers playing surrogate teachers. This seems to occur because students lack collaborative models of interaction and because teachers fail to clarify for themselves and their students the distinctive nature of collaboration in response groups.

Consequently, students ape the teacher, overlooking the strengths of real teachers' behavior and emulating the weaknesses. Brent, for example, in addition to correcting everyone's spelling and grammar, resolves questions by quoting "the rules":

> Some paragraphs can be only one word. "No." Period. That can be a paragraph. . . . In business writing you're supposed to have paragraphs be at least three sentences, but in creative writing . . .

Comments like these not only enforce superficial readings, they also prevent open-ended group inquiry into more substantive engagement with ideas. In Freire's terms, Brent forestalls dialogue by simply "depositing" his ideas on others.

In their role as surrogate teacher, readers also tend to identify problems in their "students' " work, but they either leave the "student" to solve the problem alone or they give vague, sometimes incorrect advice. One of the high school teachers I've worked with voiced the fairly common concern that group revision sessions in her classes sometimes resulted in rewritings that were *worse* than the original, leaving her in the position of undermining the group's work if she corrected their corrections. The same sort of problem surfaces in one of the groups of college writers we have been following. As the group reviews Kate's paper, Carl suggests, "Maybe do a little experimentation with that sentence, maybe change it around." Kate responds, "I could say here, 'They get sarcastic when they get tired and they don't want to do anything and they blame it on me.' Is that unclear? Do I kind of lose it?" Unfortunately, Carl agrees that the new sentence is perfectly clear, and Linda breaks in with a suggestion for improving a sentence on another page. Imagine poor Kate's consternation when she got back the original sentence from her instructor.

With his call for experimentation, Carl imitates the form but not the substance of a teacher's role. He rewards Kate not for the correctness of her response (indeed he seems to have stopped listening to the substance of it) but, as teachers often do, for trying at all. As the "student" in this relationship,

Kate accepts her "teacher's" judgment. Meanwhile Linda, Carl's colleague, politely avoids eavesdropping on his instruction, waiting instead to take up her role as instructor—by pointing out another detail that could be improved. Like their real role models, these students recognize the value of blending praise with criticism and rewarding efforts, but they fail to fulfill the other half of this role, that of guiding and shaping those efforts. They are so entrenched in the teacher stereotype they fail to perceive and practice alternative kinds of interaction.

Writers seem as eager to play student as readers do to play teacher. Writers do take the initiative of opening most review sessions, first by apologizing for their work and seeking reassurance and then by asking such general questions as "What did you think of X?" "Did Y flow?" "Was Z clear?" Soon, however, they assume a more passive stance. They often behave defensively, much as they do with actual teachers—explaining their intentions only after questions have been raised, waiting for weaknesses to be found out, seldom serving as critics of their own work, rarely guiding the discussion toward issues or problems they need to have resolved.

Even when they ask their group for response, writers usually fail to raise pointed, specific questions or to persist in asking questions until they get the responses they need. As the questions above indicate, they may press weakly for comments on clarity, organization, and development, but they essentially seem to see their role as recording the more informed opinions of their surrogate teachers, the student readers.

Based on these assumptions about their roles, students engage in discussion randomly: an anxious, staccato succession of unrelated comments from readers, followed by the writer's acknowledgment of the comment, sometimes a tentative response or partial explanation of intent, and then the introduction of another issue by another reader. The exchanges reflect the interaction patterns learned from predominantly teacher-centered discussions prevalent at every grade level, in every subject. Students go through the motions of discussion, "scoring points" by making original oral contributions rather than responding to, challenging, amplifying, or qualifying someone else's remark. So intent is each student on saying his or her piece that they fail even to listen to each other, much less engage in the collaborative weaving of meaning characteristic of more democratic group structures.

Carrying these habits into their peer groups, student/writers sometimes respond to their teacher/readers by paraphrasing the advice they receive ("So sorta expand that part a little bit?" "I should explain more of the things?"), but they rarely use concrete language to anchor these generalities to specifics in the text, nor do other readers follow up on these suggestions. Instead, readers seem to have absorbed the worst features of their teachers' grading habits—the vague admonitions to "develop" ideas or clean up and smooth out "awkward" sentences—while writers respond as if they know what these suggestions mean and how to implement them. Much discussion in response groups grows out of these poorly realized roles; it does little more than signal to writers that a particular sentence may need some more work later on—useful but limited information.

Summing up the character of much student interaction, James Moffett observes that young writers "can spot writing problems very well, but often they do not have enough understanding of the cause of a problem to know how to solve it. This insufficient understanding more than anything else causes them to pick at each other's papers in a faultfinding spirit or to make shallow suggestions for change."[1] Moffett attributes this behavior to immaturity and egocentric thinking, which keep student writers from seeing fully perspectives other than their own. Though he is surely correct in identifying the shallowness and faultfinding of students' responses to their peers' work, the shortcomings in their interaction probably originate from more than insufficient understanding of written texts. Equally if not more important is students' inexperience with collaborative relationships. Not knowing how to behave in collaborative ways, students assume what they perceive as the didactic relationship of teacher to student, which largely determines the nature and quality of their responses to each other's drafts.

Toward Collaborative Interaction

For peer interaction, the stereotypical roles of teacher and student are insufficient. In fact, they can be downright destructive of the give-and-take needed to bring about insightful invention and revision. What students need is information about the nature of collaborative interaction and opportunities to practice it. They also need to become aware that they have chosen to play some clearly defined roles, that these roles have determined both the students' behavior and the outcomes of group discussion, and that there are equally clear, alternative roles to choose. This self-reflective awareness involves the kind of thinking that allows students to look beyond tasks to the processes of accomplishing them and to perceive connections between interpersonal processes and composing processes: What are we doing?, how are we doing it? and what else might we do?

In collaborative relationships, students explore and resolve ideas together. Writers share with readers the responsibility for generating and testing ideas, while readers serve not just as an assembly of disparate "teachers," but as a group that works together to pool opinions and reactions, explore differences, and come to conclusions. The salient feature of group interaction, obscured by students' misappropriated roles, is sustained, goal-directed discussion characterized by critical inquiry (in the non-pejorative sense), mutual refinement of ideas, and collaborative input. (See Figure 1.)

FIGURE 1

TEACHER SURROGATE *VS.* PEER COLLABORATOR
The Problem of Role Definition in Writing Groups

Characteristics of the
Teacher Surrogate

directive: responsible for setting
group task and achieving results

supremely knowledgeable; in
possession of "right" answers,
"rules," "good advice"

identifies problems but fails to
take an active role in revising

Student Role

passive recording of more informed
opinions

shortcomings should be "discovered" by authority, not
"revealed" by student

non-critical toward self

Interaction Pattern

random, staccato interaction:
question/answer format or
"skyrocketing"

Characteristics of the
Peer Collaborator

mutual generation and exploration
of ideas

equal status relationships;
non-hierarchical

shared leadership functions:
  initiating
  regulating
  informing
  supporting
  evaluating

shared responsibility for achieving
group task

reflexive awareness of group process
and quality of outcomes

Interaction Pattern

sustained, goal-directed discussion

decision-making by consensus or
merit, not by authority

Contrast, for example, the qualities of peer interaction in many of the
previous excerpts with those of a discussion between a "real" teacher and
student, reported in Thomas Carnicelli's essay on the writing conference:

STUDENT: Well . . . I have so much to say about my music because I've
done quite a few things, and so it's really crammed. I could've written
a lot more, with more interesting things.

TEACHER: I think you've really hit the nail on the head. What you've got
here is almost a short chronology of all the things you've done, and I
don't think that's the thing you really want us to know about: "Should
I go on?"–your music and how you feel about it. I mean, the title is

"A Life of Music?" and you don't really address that as much as you could have. I think it's really interesting to see your varied experiences and how professional they really were, but I think you could tighten that section way down.

STUDENT: I think with a five-page paper . . . or it would take about a ten-page paper, easily.

TEACHER: Yeah, but I'd want you to focus in, though. There's so much in this paper. Why did you decide not to go to Emerson? I think that's something you could tell us more about.[2]

This discussion shows many characteristics of collaborative interaction. The reader shares responsibility for the content of the revised piece, not only in asking questions and making suggestions, but in thinking through new possibilities *with* the writer. The concreteness of the discussion is also noteworthy. It leads to a more focused exploration of the text's shortcomings and its latent possibilities than is evident in the peer interaction examined so far. The teacher/reader has been able to identify the key shortcoming of the draft. Further, she supports her finding by recalling details from the draft, then begins helping the writer identify potential central ideas around which to revise the draft. This interchange also blends positive with negative comments, but in contrast with students' fears it does so without embarrassing the writer. The reader considers the paper on its own merits rather than resorting to rules or prescriptions about "good writing."

In addition, the focus is on concepts rather than words and phrases. Missing are the egocentric personal associations that allow discussion to drift from point to point. Instead, the discussion remains centered on the text with ideas for development coming from issues the writer has begun to acknowledge already.

This excerpt also has direction, showing a search for pattern that will organize and unify the discrete items that arise. The conversation develops out of an awareness not just of the task of revising, but of its own progress in achieving that task. In other words, the teacher is aware of how the conference is progressing and uses that perspective to assess, clarify, and direct the task. Reading the text and reading its "context" become complementary processes. Without this metaperspective on discussion, participants drift out of control, at the mercy of whatever currents emerge. Only twice, for instance, in the transcript in Chapter 2, does someone prompt the group to get back to the paper—a rather unsophisticated perspective on maintenance-level problems. More often, readers simply meander around the topic, leaving writers to make of the discussion what they will.

Sometimes, comments on a group's performance overtly reflect an awareness of the group's behavior, as in this excerpt:

WRITER: I don't know why I tried to put this together this way. I don't
think it's worth taking up our time. Why don't we go ahead and talk
about Joan's piece?

READER: No, let's look at it. We do our best stuff when somebody has
something that's a little off the wall.

Here, the reader's response directs the group's attention to one of the patterns of their discussion, suggesting and then elaborating on how the part fits
with the whole. Equally effective—though more subtle—are comments that
call for a culmination or synthesis of previous issues, directed toward a next
step. Responses of this sort knit discussion together to give the whole interaction direction and purpose:

READER: So I just get kind of lost in the story. I don't know what to make
of it even though I like a lot of the details.

WRITER: Yeah, I just have a lot of scattered incidents.

READER: Well, what's the thing you should focus on? I thought the part
where you talked about everyone being worried about you was something I'd like to hear more about.

WRITER: Yeah, I think that starts to pull it together. How about . . .?

Here, the reader keeps the discussion going by helping the writer clarify
ideas that will be refined in the next draft. The emphasis, again, is conceptual
rather than lexical, and continuous rather than piecemeal.

Students need to "unlearn" the tendency to behave like teachers in a
collaborative situation. In good discussions, readers are simultaneously aware
of the text, the task, and the direction of their discussion. They share responsibility for revising the text and conduct the discussion so the writer comes
away with a clear sense of what and how to revise. Thus, by becoming aware
of and controlling their group interaction, participants practice the generic
cognitive skills of making connections, articulating contrasts, forming conclusions, integrating, and synthesizing. These skills underlie successful collaboration in groups as well as meaningful, worthwhile writing.

Leadership Patterns in Collaborative Groups

To work collaboratively, students need to understand something of the
nature of leadership in groups. Teacher surrogates exercise the wrong kind.
They force other members into a passive role, but they lack the knowledge
and instructional ability to make that passivity worthwhile. In other words,
they can't deliver what they promise. Nor is it a good gamble for teachers to
appoint leaders by predicting intuitively which of their students will succeed
in both managing the discussion and providing guidance to the members. In

the Utah Plan, the project mentioned in Chapter 2, ten student discussion leaders were appointed by an experienced sociologist after he conducted personal interviews with the candidates and with their former teachers. Only two students thus selected were successful.

The most natural leader in student groups is the writer, since the other group members are particularly sensitive to embarassing or discomfiting the person whose ideas are being "criticized." Groups need permission from writers to review their work. By learning to accept this role rather than evasively opting to play student, writers can begin to move their groups toward mature collaboration.

When writers become leaders, they don't "lead" in the conventional sense. They must become less directive and more facilitative, since they are leaders who are seeking advice and collecting responses, not giving help. The leader may not even be fully aware of the problems the group needs to explore; their task is to identify problems and devise solutions collectively. Since such leaders can't singlehandedly control the group's task, they must instead learn to mediate the processes through which the group works. Moreover, as leadership functions shift from one writer to the next, groups learn not to look to a single, perhaps overbearing person to give guidance and direction. This shifting leadership establishes a workable middle ground from which mature group leadership can evolve—not leadership invested in a single leader but leadership as a function dispersed among all members of the group.

This model is consistent with much of what we know from research into group organization. In *Learning to Work in Groups,* Matthew Miles summarizes much of this research with his list of five crucial functions for group leadership:

> initiating
> regulating
> informing
> supporting
> evaluating[3]

These functions refer to both the group's task and its behavior in carrying it out. Without leadership that reflects all five functions, groups flounder.

For the most part, writers succeed in initiating the exploration of ideas or reviews of drafts, but the other four leadership functions are usually absent. These functions depend on the group's ability to think about their own behavior: to regulate pace, to keep the group informed about how it's doing, to support members by listening and providing appropriate feedback, and to evaluate the group's effectiveness. The mature group, as one investigator describes it, "constantly tests its conclusions in a scientific spirit. It seeks out knowledge, learns from experience, and constantly questions how it may best achieve its goal. It is clearly conscious of . . . the processes of learning and development."[4]

This description emphasizes the necessary balance of task and maintenance functions in groups—a balance that is missing in many of the transcripts presented so far. Students need a basic understanding of how these leadership functions support the collaborative nature of group work. They need to understand what people do to regulate or support group work and to see how this makes communication possible. Further, they need chances to practice these behaviors in helping each other invent and revise ideas so they can recognize the important connections with writing.

The Milgram experiments on obedience to authority provide some useful insights into just what might be needed to develop collaborative group relationships. In these experiments, participants were instructed to deliver increasingly stronger electrical shocks to their "partners" as punishment for error. Even though the shocks presumably reached crippling intensities, many experimental subjects were unable to contradict the experimenter and reject the terms of the experiment. Almost no one walked out of the experiment; and only a few subjects even exercised a form of passive resistance by refusing to obey instructions by remaining seated until dismissed.

The subjects of the experiment weren't "bad" people; none of them condoned inflicting pain on others. But in a face-to-face encounter with someone who demanded that they live up to the experiment's agreed-upon conditions, they caved in—despite their convictions. Groups, too, exert pressure on members to follow the group will, and the Milgram experiments provide some clues about what individuals may need to resist pressure to conform.

In an analysis of the Milgram research, John Sabini and Maury Silver argue convincingly that the incidence of passive resistance among the subjects suggests that people simply don't know how to say no.[5] Their resistance confirms that they "knew" at some level that they were being asked to do something wrong, but they didn't seem to know how to say so to the experimenter. How many of us have had much practice telling people in authority that we won't do what they tell us? How often are children and adolescents punished when they try? To be able to do so we need two things: first, we need to know what words to use, a language of resistance or alternatives. Second, we need to get our reasons to a high enough level of awareness that we can explain what is wrong and why. Neither the language nor the insight comes without practice.

Similarly, collaborative relationships in writing groups need to be nurtured. Collaborating with peers is relatively unfamiliar in comparison with the leader/follower or teacher/student relationship. Collaborative relationships may come about only when students have opportunities to anticipate sharing and integrating their ideas with others', when they can see others doing the same, and when they can practice it themselves. The Milgram experiments offer an extreme instance of the need to opt out. But they also suggest a broader context for thinking about what people need in any interpersonal situation to reconcile individual needs with group (or authority) demands, or what we know with what we do. Opportunities for reflection and practice seem crucial.

Possibility and Potential in Peer Interaction

There are strong indications that students *can* learn to work effectively in groups. I close this chapter with three examples of productive group inter-action and then move in subsequent chapters to a discussion of how we can help students develop collaborative group skills that reinforce writing. Consider this brief sketch of a successful peer discussion group:

Brad's group consisted of eight freshmen who met once or twice a week in connection with the Utah Plan. The group served partly to discuss course material, partly to provide feedback on writing, from prewriting through revising and editing. Although the group was not completely effective in revising, the students did manage to explore ideas together rather than digressing into personal associations or limiting themselves to editing. Moreover, this was an extremely powerful prewriting group that succeeded in stimulating in each member a purposeful intensity toward writing and learning.

This group gave a dominant impression of genuine warmth and caring. It was a cohesive, enthusiastic group that, through time, overcame many inhibitions about sharing ideas. Explaining their success, Steve said in several interviews during their second quarter together, "The most important thing is that we like each other." Simple as it sounds, liking and the trust that stems from it are crucial to successful peer interaction. The members were aware of having defined themselves as a group, and they appreciated their differences, having used them to add depth and variety to their exchanges.

Faced with a writing task, they devoted great energy to prewriting activities. They came to meetings with ideas more or less thought out, some knowing what they wanted to write about, some with notes or rough drafts, others unsure or doubtful of the quality of their thoughts. Primarily their strategy was to talk out their papers, verbally rehearsing ideas before committing them to writing. Ida and William Hill, in their monograph, *Learning and Teaching through Discussion,* echo Donald Murray's descriptions of discussion as a chance to "rehearse" ideas. As the students in Brad's group discovered, discussion transforms "silent verbalization" to the shared medium of talking, "which is amenable to testing, modification, and further development." [6]

In this group, the members agreed that ideas discussed verbally are easier to accept, modify, or reject; they are less permanent and easier to throw away than when they have been written down. The group identified this process as "talking out." The development of private terminology such as this gives a strong indication that they had begun to consider the methods through which the group operated. "Talking out" served as a check on an idea's interest, value, or appropriateness. The group was also willing to share ideas in what they called an "idea pool" in hopes of either making their own ideas better or of giving someone else some insights. Brad, designated the group leader from the start, exercised relatively loose control, allowing discussion to drift so long as the associations it produced seemed useful to the task. The members would joke about the tendency to digress, but nevertheless recognized it as a productive brainstorming device. Steve and Maureen helped to keep discussion in hand; in fact, the group acknowledged and respected their frequent insistence that members define their terms or rephrase what they had said.

As a result of their strength as a group, these students stimulated one another's interest in writing assignments so that their ideas became really important to themselves and each other. This strength seemed to increase each person's self-esteem and confidence. While their writing abilities ranged from very strong to low-average, they all tended to ask actively, "What do *I* want in this paper and how can I make it better?" rather than the more passive teacher-centered question, "What do *you* want?"

Bolstered by the group and personally committed to their ideas, they also tended to make healthy use of instructor feedback on drafts and final revisions. They were more ready than students in less successful groups to show their drafts to each other, to ask specific questions about them, and to solicit the teacher's feedback to complement, not substitute for peer feedback. As a result, grades became informative and descriptive for them, primarily another source of feedback. Most important, they were aware of group processes like pooling ideas and digressing, and they used this awareness to keep the group on track.

A second example of successful group work suggests that students are capable of lively and production collaboration in revision. Here, helping Sherrie come up with a title, group members demonstrate the classic features of brainstorming: free association, playfulness, non-critical attitudes, and "piggybacking" ideas—that is, elaborating on a previous idea:

SHERRIE: I couldn't think of anything.
CARRIE: "Apartment Hunting"?
SHERRIE: I just couldn't think of anything. Uh—I guess lately we've had so many hassles with our apartment . . .
JIM: "The Hassle of Apartment Living"?
SHERRIE: "The Hassle of Finding Off-Campus Living"?
BRENT: That would be true.
JIM: "The Housing Hassle"
SHERRIE: Yeah—"The Off-Campus Housing Hassle"!

Though the dialogue is restricted to finding a title, the students nevertheless engage in a vigorous sense of play with ideas and language. They start with nothing and use the group to generate an effective and satisfying title. With opportunities built into the group procedure for reflecting on their behavior, members would become more likely to recognize their success here, recount how it came about, and subsequently use that understanding to inform more of their work in revising.

The third example shows the power of peer groups in reinforcing the concept of audience. Even with the shortcomings of group behavior described throughout these chapters, groups reveal to writers this essential dimension of composing: that one writes and rewrites for audiences. Regardless of how aware of this fact students are intellectually, they seem to realize it fully only when they share their writing with actual readers. The excitement conveyed in Carol's discovery that her assumptions aren't equally clear to her readers is especially indicative:

CARL: Where it says "the appearance of the two men at the door"? Can you be more descriptive there without, uh,—Like, were they uh—paramedics, or what?—Were they doctors, or—

CAROL: Oh.

CARL: You know, maybe describe the two young men—a little better, were they in—uniforms, or . . .

CAROL: Oh, okay.

CARL: Yeah.

CAROL: I really don't know—what . . . (heh-heh) but um, yeah, I think . . . white coats on, or—I—

CARL: Yeah, just—someone looking medical, or were they the—ambulance guys, or . . .

CAROL: Is—, yeah, okay.

CARL: Besides that, you're very good at describing things.

CAROL: No, it really . . . That really helps, because a lot of times, you know, I . . . you know, you tend to take things for granted, the . . . the—audience knows—um, exactly who you're talking about without being—you know, without having to say exactly who they are. I just tend to think that everybody seems to know and—It really helps—so much, you know, you just—you say that . . . I didn't know who you were talking about.

KATE: Well, I think (pause). Except—for the situation, I don't think you really needed to know who they were.

CAROL: Well—the part that—I mean, it could've been—I mean, they could've been just . . . They could've been two more—people waiting for—you know, to go to the waiting room.

KATE: That's what I thought at first. But then . . .

Note that Carol is not the only one to discover something about the audience. Kate, too, seems to realize that she may have taken too much for granted in her first reading.

CAROL: Yeah, I didn't even think of that.

CARL: I thought it'd just make it a little more clearer, 'cause uh . . . lot of times it may have been like one of these ambulance guys or—doctors—or—

CAROL: Oh.

CARL: I—I didn't think maybe the paramedics would be the ones who would give you the news, I thought maybe it might be the doctors.

CAROL: Oh.

CARL: So I thought it might be a little more clearer if you . . .

CAROL: Okay.

Carol's responses suggest two things: first, she has made an important connection between what she has been taught about writing and what she has just experienced about her own writing. Second, she has begun to project herself into the audience's perspective by seeing the ambiguity as someone else might and thinking aloud how they might have understood the sentence.

Once this awareness sinks in, students become more likely to compose alternative constructions aloud, using the group as a sounding board. Unlike composing sentences in private, oral composition in groups seems to capitalize on the writer's projected self as she hears her words the way her audience does. Even if peer feedback is minimal or poor, the projected self seems to provide some of its own feedback; one hears not just as oneself but in another, enlarged role. Another student made a similar discovery: "I didn't realize until just now when I was reading it out loud that I could use a lot more description in here. That's pretty neat!" Inner and outer speech begin to connect, making thoughts more consciously available to the writer as they become part of public discourse. Toby Fulwiler explains the connection this way:

> The key to understanding lies in our ability to manipulate internally information and ideas received piecemeal from external sources and give them coherent verbal shape. We learn by processing and we process by talking—to ourselves and to others. . . . We carry on conversations with friends in order to explain things to ourselves.[7]

Hearing one's sentences with others or composing them for the group begins the process of translation from inner to outer speech—one of the most fundamental reasons for peer interaction throughout the composing process.

These examples suggest the rich possibilities for student writing in groups—not just for improving clarity or correctness, and not just as a peculiarity of school life—but for cultivating the conceptual and rhetorical arenas in which writing must function to be valued as a significant human activity. From this standpoint, the use of peer response groups is more than a pedagogical technique; it is a representation of one's philosophy concerning the nature and purpose of writing.

The problems students experience in developing their writing collaboratively are an extension of their difficulties with writing itself. Problems with writing, like problems with peer interaction, spring from the same sources. Both sets of problems are solvable, however, reducible as they are to behaviors that can be identified, isolated, practiced, and refined. The best way to begin is to recognize with our students that response groups are hard work, that we have to learn together how to shape them in ways that work best for us. The following chapters are designed to help response groups take shape. They clarify the nature of process as it occurs in the parallel activities of writing, learning, and interacting, and suggest methods for helping students develop reading, listening, and feedback skills that link all three areas.

Notes

1.   James Moffett, *Teaching the Universe of Discourse* (Boston: Houghton Mifflin, 1968), p. 196.
2.   Thomas Carnicelli, "The Writing Conference: A One-to-One Conversation," in *Eight Approaches to Teaching Composition,* Timothy R. Donovan and Ben W. McClelland, eds. (Urbana, Illinois: NCTE, 1980), p. 120.
3.   Matthew Miles, *Learning to Work in Groups: A Practical Guide for Members and Trainers,* 2nd ed. (New York: Teachers College Press, 1981).
4.   Margaret Rioch, "The Work of Wilfred Bion on Groups," in *Group Relations Reader,* Arthur D. Coleman and W. Harold Benton, eds. (San Rafael, California: Associates Printing & Publishing Co., 1975), p. 29.
5.   John Sabini and Maury Silver, "Critical Thinking and Obedience to Authority," *National Forum* 65 (Winter 1985), pp. 13–17.
6.   Ida and William Hill, *Learning and Teaching Through Discussion,* (Center for the Study of Liberal Education for Adults, 1958), p. 8.
7.   Toby Fulwiler, "Writing: An Act of Cognition," in *Teaching Writing in All Disciplines,* C. William Griffin, ed. (San Francisco: Jossey-Bass, 1982), p. 17.

PART II

Developing Productive
Peer Response Groups

6

A Successful
Revision Session

I began with an annotated transcript of a revision session; it was a disappointing illustration of students' many failures to help each other revise in meaningful ways. We now see something of the logic behind students' difficulties—why sharing writing poses problems for many students. Those problems, however, also show why the process of sharing writing is vitally important, not just in yielding better written products, but in generating the thinking, reading, and interpersonal abilities that are also essential. The transcript in this chapter counterbalances the earlier one. It is a model of what to look for in a productive revision session, and it is also a touchstone for subsequent chapters that provide help in developing effective writing groups.

The six students in this group are juniors and seniors, English education majors who were members of a methods course on teaching writing. They have had about as much or less formal instruction in writing as the students in the earlier transcripts, and they are all just beginning their coursework in education. They represent average writing and group discussion abilities of college juniors and seniors.

Throughout the term this group had debated and discussed the value of peer response; everyone had experienced as a participant in previous group situations most of the problems I have been describing, and a few maintained considerable skepticism about the practice of peer response—no matter how persuasive they found the theory. The students had done some research on group learning, both in general and in writing classes, but they hadn't practiced any particular techniques. The transcript I include here represents their first attempt to try out what they had learned from reading and talking about the process of sharing writing.

The group is discussing Audrey's draft of the first two pages of a three-week unit plan. I have deleted some discussion in the interest of space and readability but have tried to preserve its flavor and progression.

71

AUDREY: I'll tell you where I had problems, maybe that could start it off. Some questions I had. But I'll let those other guys reread it again.

Audrey accepts responsibility for initiating the discussion, implicitly inviting the group to review and analyze her draft.

(pause while students reread draft)

KAREN: How long is their speech?

AUDREY: Oh, I'd say five to 15 minutes.

KAREN: And you're going to work that out the whole year?

AUDREY: No. What I'm going to do is—that is going to be the introductory unit. Say I'll teach it maybe the second week of school. It's a fairly long unit. It's a two- or three-week unit, and then what I'll do is, um, teach this unit so I can start the students out by getting them in groups, by getting them to identify their role as a learner and by getting them started on a file-type thing for their writing. And then I'll take this space, this two-week space and, say, have mini-lessons every day or, you know, writing exercises, or integrate writing every single day, if it's journal writing, free writing type of writing. Maybe not every single day—that may be too idealistic—maybe every other day or twice a week. Some type of writing process or some type of writing skill type thing, and then work on it—have them hand it in and see what their problems are, hand it back to 'em and work on those specific things like fragments or infinitives or whatever.

KAREN: OK. So participate in group discussion this whole year?

Karen paraphrases what she thinks Audrey intends to suggest in the draft, giving Audrey a chance to clarify herself.

AUDREY: No, they . . . No. No. This isn't the whole year. This is for the unit. OK?

KAREN: OK.

AUDREY: Now, uh . . .

KAREN: The unit is for the whole year. The first page is the whole year. What you plan on doing.

AUDREY: Uh huh.

KAREN: What you want them to do . . . No?

AUDREY: Yeah. That's what I want 'em to do. I want 'em to have responsibilities, you know, I'd get—I never thought of it that way.

Audrey begins to recognize the ambiguity in her draft. Her willingness to admit it also allows Karen to pursue her questions.

KAREN: I don't understand.

AUDREY: OK.

KAREN: I got the idea that you wanted to do this the whole year long and these were some of the things they were gonna do throughout the year.

AUDREY: No. All right. The overall objectives will be the whole year-type objectives. OK? Maybe.

Audrey's "maybe" suggests that she is not just thinking about how to "fix" the draft but is beginning to reconceptualize the unit. This process continues throughout the discussion.

KAREN: OK, then, what the students are expected to do in the unit . . .

AUDREY: . . . in the unit is in these two weeks. It may end up being a three-week unit because there's a lot of stuff in there.

KAREN: OK. But the I AM book is the whole year, isn't it?

Karen continues to paraphrase, and Audrey's ability to complete Karen's sentence suggests that they are beginning to think and talk about the same things.

AUDREY: Um, it will be a continuous process so they will keep adding to it. I'd like 'em to all have file folders of their writing.

AGGIE: Do you think they will be able to, uh, present their point of view that they may take when they are 40?

AUDREY: Yeah, I think they will.

AGGIE: Yeah?

Aggie raises the first question about the validity of one of Audrey's ideas, but rather than judging it she nudges Audrey to think about it. This issue becomes the focal point of the session, although the group is not yet ready to deal with it explicitly.

AUDREY: I think—just think like your parents or what, what would your parents write at this point?

LORI: OK, now could you give an example of something they could do for a demonstration speech?

Lori pulls away from Aggie's implied criticism by changing the subject and asking for an example as a way to clarify another ambiguity.

AUDREY: Um. I thought, you know, if, say, all right, say I play tennis a lot, OK? I would just maybe demonstrate how to serve or how to do a backhand.

LORI: OK.

AUDREY: You know, something like that—just something that they're interested in so that the students are getting to know each other, being relaxed around each other and having some type of group dynamics working at the very, very first of the year. That's what I want to do—is—is get this group, class-as-a-whole feeling and very comfortable feeling right at the first of the year so that the students know exactly what's expected of them. I mean, I want to teach this thing on "the students will identify their role as learner"—I want to teach that during that unit so that they know what their responsibility is as a learner.

LORI: OK, so it's really kind of like, kind of like a special—specialization speech, something they specialize in.

AUDREY: Yeah. Yeah.

LORI: I think your wording could probably be a little bit better there because I was confused about some dramatic event like my father dying or something.

Having made sure she understands fully what Audrey's intentions are, Lori suggests a clarification in the text. Significantly, she anchors her suggestion in her own confusion, not in Audrey's "error" for not having done it right the first time.

AUDREY: Oh, OK.

LORI: Yeah, I was confused about that.

LORI: So now, how are you going to get kids to "identify their role as a learner within the school system"?

Lori opens up a new problem with the draft by asking Audrey to look at it in terms of how she might go about applying the idea. Her continued use of questions is useful in helping Audrey rethink and explain the idea. Thus, the group situation helps Audrey articulate her revised ideas before she tries revising in writing.

AUDREY: What I'd like to do is, um, do some type of demonstration with— I don't know whether it's gonna be with the students or what—that will teach them role identification as a police officer, role identification as a grocery clerk, but see, you know, you know, you fulfill certain roles through your daily life. I mean, I go to work, I'm something; go to class, I'm something else. And so maybe what I'd like to do is have an act-out type role—role playing situation and set it up with the students in the class, set it up with someone else and bring them in and then act that out and have them say, "OK. What type of roles did these people take? What type of roles?" And maybe you could do parent/child roles.

KAREN: You could even do "and why?"

Karen collaborates with Audrey by thinking along with her and offering an extension on her initial idea.

AUDREY: Yeah, that's a good idea.

LORI: And even a movie could be good for that. It would really demonstrate the certain kind of role . . .

Lori continues "piggybacking" on Audrey's idea by adding another relevant suggestion.

AUDREY: Uh humm. Yeah. And then talk to them about roles and talk to them about responsibility and what types of responsibility they have as learners. What types of responsibility they have as children. All right. Give them several examples—children in the family, how many of them work, what type of responsibilities do you have then? All right. Do you take more responsibility on yourself as an employee just because you make money than you do as a learner? Yeah, you do. And so, where do you draw the line? Where does that—where do you have that responsibility?

These suggestions help Audrey think more concretely about possibilities she had not initially imagined.

SALLY: OK. Now see, I'd have a problem there because I never worked when I was in high school.

Sally, also thinking along with the others, anticipates another problem. Her response derives from empathetic thinking and demonstrates another aspect of challenging feedback. (See Chapter 10.)

AUDREY: OK.

SALLY: Let me tell you—but I was the youngest child. So I think you could say so where was my responsibility out there?

AUDREY: Yeah—uh, responsibility in other organizations: if you're on a team, a cheerleader; your responsibilities, uh, in your religion, responsibilities as a citizen, you know.

KAREN: Would that be hard to put all that you just said into your papers if a substitute were to come and read, "Today we're gonna identify our role as learners"? She'd say, "What???"

*Karen uses what she knows about role playing for shifting point
of view by asking Audrey to look at her unit plan from the perspective of a substitute teacher.*

AUDREY: (laughing) I'd sure as hell try to be there. You know . . .
KAREN: 'Cause I don't exactly understand that either. Couldn't you expand
    on that objective?
AUDREY: Yeah.
KAREN: . . . and say exactly what you want?

*Audrey is feeling comfortable enough to accept Karen's criticism
but also to explain her reasons and to distinguish between writing
for herself and writing for someone else. She does not just passively take in the feedback being given, nor does she argue with it
defensively and dismiss it.*

AUDREY: The reason I put it like the overall objective is—all right, say I
    have these overall objectives and they're, they're based on Bloom's
    taxonomy, by the way, they, they are progressive, that's why there's
    six of them. You start out with knowledge and um, the reason that I
    did it this way is because, all right, I can identify with them and this
    is my own thing, all right? But, and I mean if I was going to give my
    unit to you I would probably expand more on that because I would
    be giving it to someone else. I agree with you on that. I'll probably
    expand more on it, or just attach something. But, see, I know what I
    want to do there. But I need to . . .
LORI: Yeah.
AUDREY: Definitely explain a little more . . .
LORI: Get into the *how's* and things like that.

*Lori paraphrases with Audrey the revisions she needs to think
about, but she is also careful to acknowledge what she sees as
the strengths of the draft.*

AUDREY: OK.
LORI: It's great, though, what you've described. It really . . .
AUDREY: OK, so what I need to do, then, is just add more to my objectives,
    my overall objectives . . . examples . . .

*Audrey summarizes the group's suggestions to be sure she under-
stands them and to give the group a chance for further clarification.*

KAREN: I don't know. I just read that paper that she gave me on revising
    [Nancy Sommers' 1980 essay] and it seems like one of the main

things professional writers do is that they try to grasp the form of what they mean.

Karen draws on outside readings to put the problem in a more informed perspective.

AUDREY: Uh huh.

KAREN: . . . and put that in. But when you just have "students will identify their roles as learner" you don't really have a form, you're just
saying . . .

AUDREY: You can't see it, can you?

Audrey's question is a good example of empathic understanding of Karen's confusion.

KAREN: No.

AUDREY: OK.

KAREN: It needs to be bigger.

AUDREY: So, I need to put in *how's* on all my objectives, right?

LORI: It's real interesting to me how 2 follows 1, because 2 seems like that
would come first.

With Audrey's direct acknowledgement of the group's confusion, Lori feels freer to offer some explicit suggestions. She challenges Audrey's idea, again by putting it in terms of her own response, but not a rule or imperative for Audrey to follow.

AUDREY: Really?

LORI: Yeah. 'Cause it seems like you could look at "where do I fit in my
family?" That's much easier to understand, that's much less abstract
than "How do I fit in as a learner"—I mean, you just don't think about
that.

AUDREY: Maybe what I was doing, maybe what I could do is just take out
the #2.

Now fully collaborating with Lori, Audrey responds by trying out in concrete terms a way to resolve Lori's question.

LORI: Yeah.

AUDREY: And, uh, go from, just add that on to #2? Would that be better?

LORI: Yeah—or, and, and change the wording "Translate this identity . . ."

Lori too, gets involved in rethinking the idea and rewording the draft.

'Cause it seems like identifying first with my family and all that comes first.

AUDREY: OK. Maybe that they will, uh . . .

LORI: 'Cause I really like how your ideas are developing. Having someone come in or seeing a movie or something and to look at someone else's role that is apart from them and then . . .

Lori's comment reflects her awareness of the process *of evolving meaning.*

AUDREY: I felt that that's a lot easier to teach through pulling them back and OK, "this is just another example of a role." OK, "do you see this?" Now . . .

KAREN: Couldn't that be part of their demonstration project? I mean, you have employment here:

Karen helps to maintain the coherence of the discussion by recalling an earlier problem and making a connection with the current issue.

"I'm a checker": you mentioned grocery stores. I could get up and tell them about: "My role at work is . . .," you know, and you do what you're told; you're always here and you're always there. And then that would be a—I would be identifying a different role for me.

Audrey picks up the idea and elaborates on it; her elaboration deepens her understanding of what students might gain from her proposed exercise.

AUDREY: Well, and, and, also you know, say that, say for example, the checker. When I was a checker, when I was training for it, I was amazed at all the things that a checker does. Like, what you look for on a check, uh, how you do, you know, all the buttons that you push and all the look-up codes for produce and stuff like that. I was amazed and I think that would be helpful—you know, I could probably help the students integrate those specific things. So when you change the oil in a car if you work for Minute Lube—all the things you do. So. Yeah, you know, this first objective could work into that demonstration speech. Definitely.

LAUREL: You know, what might be also interesting is at the end of this autobiography that they're going to end up with, um, are they going to then compile it at the end by looking at everything or are you planning on having them start out with, you know, "Write a paragraph on what's important to you right now?" "What is your goal?" And then take that away from them and stick it in a folder so they can't see and have them rewrite it at the end, "Now what I want you to write today is where are you?" "What's important?" "How do you feel about it?" And then hand them back out . . .

Laurel, too, is thinking collaboratively with Audrey, so her suggestion maintains the spirit of Audrey's goal for the unit plan.

AUDREY: That's a good idea.

LORI: That's a great idea!

LAUREL: Because if it's in there all the time, they're liable to just, you know, they can look at it, and . . .

Audrey extends the implications of Laurel's suggestion.

AUDREY: Just start out the unit like that and then pull it and then have them write different pieces of their own autobiography and then go and pull it?

Audrey and Karen's enthusiastic responses suggest that the group is thinking together about the draft and its subject.

LAUREL: Yeah. You keep it. You keep the original writing so they can't look back at it and draw from it and then at the end of the unit or even the end of the year, have them write the exact same thing, give them exactly the same instructions and see how their writing has changed, how their views have changed, how they've grown as a person.

AUDREY: That a *good* idea!

KAREN: That's a *real* good idea!

AUDREY: Do you think maybe you could even do that—say, start out the unit or the year with that and then after that unit have 'em write another one and then save both of 'em and the, say, after the term, have 'em write something else? I mean, because you know it'd be simple—just a paragraph—something simple.

SALLY: Yeah. And you always remember those kind of questions.

AUDREY: "Bang, bang, bang," say do it four or five times. And then say from the start, then take the first one they ever wrote at the beginning of the year . . .

LAUREL: I think it would be more significant than the point of view when they're 40 because all they have . . .

AUDREY: I agree with you.

LAUREL: . . . to rely on is their parents and they're not their parents.

AUDREY: I agree with you.

Having "tested the waters," Laurel finds it safe enough to dive in with her "real" suggestion—that Audrey reconsider her idea of having students write a projective essay. This was the idea that Aggie initially challenged. By now Audrey is ready to rethink its validity, and she paraphrases Laurel's statement to make sure she is picking up the real message.

LAUREL: You know, you really can't project what you're going to be doing in the future. It would be just science fiction to do it.

AUDREY: So, what you want me to do is just keep it more at the present day, we just start say at the first of the two weeks and then—or three weeks—and then three weeks later—I mean, that seems more now to them; I mean, they're not worried about what it's like to be 40.

LAUREL: Show 'em their growth. Say, "Now look at the two papers you have in front of you. You wrote this one the first week of class, the first day of class, and this is what you said.

AUDREY: Uh hmm.

LAUREL: And look at what you've written now after three weeks of class.

AUDREY: Oh. OK.

LAUREL: You know, keep pulling those papers. Don't let them keep them in their folders so they can't keep looking at them.

AUDREY: I like that a lot better because . . .

LORI: I like the 40 idea, too, though because I think it's really neat for kids, well, you know, what's the course of your life up until you're like maybe even 30 is probably better.

AUDREY: Closer to their age.

LORI: Yeah, because I did that when I was a junior in high school and it was really fun because I'd never really thought about it. What did I want to do? I think Laurel's been thinking a little more practical.

AUDREY: Yeah, yeah, but I like this idea, too.

LORI: I like that idea too. I can't see why they couldn't both work.

Rather than getting swept up by the new idea, Lori defends the original theme topic. The group discovers that it is the right idea, but maybe in the wrong place, for the wrong reason.

AUDREY: Yeah, I think we could integrate them.

LAUREL: Well, I like the idea of the 40s simply because it would be a fun thing to write, but I don't think the progression would be right because it would be all projection, it would all be guessing.

AUDREY: Maybe I could use that later on.

LAUREL: You could use it as something else, but I don't think . . .

LORI: It would sure be fun though.

LAUREL: OK. I have to leave.

AUDREY: So what type—all right. You wanted goals, how they feel about their life now. What else could you put in that paragraph? Some more concrete things.

With Laurel getting ready to leave, Audrey insists on a degree of closure by summarizing Laurel's suggestion and asking for "more concrete things."

LAUREL: "What's important for you today?" "What do you think you might get out of this class?"

AUDREY: That'd be an interesting thing.

LAUREL: "What's your favorite class?" because sometimes I know that my favorite class at the beginning of a quarter is not my favorite class at the end.

From the standpoint of content as well as process, this was an effective revision session. The group quickly focused on Audrey's chief writing problem—lack of concreteness—a problem she was confronted with for the first time during this course. Rather than simply trying to fix Audrey's draft by tinkering with wording or sentence structure, the group probes for a clearer statement of Audrey's goals and proposed methods. When the group has reached a common understanding of her intentions, they collectively assume the problem of thinking it through with her. Their suggestions and criticisms are thus consistent with the norms of the draft, and this consistency seems to enable the group to stick with the topic, to pursue concrete suggestions, and to give and receive criticisms non-defensively.

The group members also practice their knowledge of interaction skills quite naturally and comfortably. Audrey readily paraphrases and summarizes her peers' comments and frequently insists on a definite statement of the changes she needs to make before allowing the group to move on to another issue. Her readers, aware of the features of poor group revision sessions, seem careful to give useful feedback. Lori rather skillfully suggests revisions in rethinking together with rewording; Karen offers another point of view to help Audrey see the problems with her draft from a new perspective; Sally tries out ideas imaginatively and challenges their appropriateness; Laurel introduces the most severe criticism of the discussion but balances the criticism by providing an alternative. All the members are admirably careful to ground their criticisms in their own readings and reactions, giving Audrey a chance to clarify misreadings or misunderstandings. In short, they use their knowledge of effective group process to sustain a rigorous but humane revision session.

Perhaps the most cogent analysis of this session comes from the seventh member of the group, Diane, who observed the discussion and offered these comments at the end. I include them here to give teachers and their students a good model of an observer's report:

OK. I thought it was a very helpful revision session, but Audrey's the one who needs to see it that way. First of all, I thought Karen started out by asking for specifics and clarification: "how long was the speech?" specific criteria, which was probably very helpful. And then Aggie's question about "will they be able to write something about when they are 40 or will that be too hard?" That is what you really ended up with. In the end the alternative turned out to be what I think you, Audrey, agreed, and everyone else agreed would probably be a more relevant assignment. Aggie just raised that question, and then it was forgotten for a while, and then people came back to it. I guess maybe it was in other people's minds.

Lori, I thought, um, did a lot of questioning or wanting—eliciting—other explanations, or wanting other solutions, other alternatives, defining terms, other resources, questions about sequencing and things that were important there and that you need to clarify, which you did. And then when you said that it was based on Bloom's taxonomy, um, I thought that was good that you had a basis for what you were doing and had based it on something like that, and you were able to give a rationale for your reasons for doing it a certain way.

Sally made some comments about the relevance of the assignments that, you know, she had personal experience with and that she thought that they would be very good later in life. And also, I think she cited some exceptions using challenging feedback. She said, "but what about me; I didn't have a job in high school"—or something. So then that opened up the opportunity for offering wider options in your assignments which, you know, they came up with suggestions and you did, too.

I think that those are the main things that I observed. A lot of people were into clarification, expanding the options and making it a relevant unit, which it seems like it really is, because—especially keeping the file. Everyone agreed that was a good idea to see your own progress—that's *really* helpful to a student. And overall it seems to me to be, I don't know, pretty logical and pretty helpful.

I thought it was supportive and positive. I didn't sense any people being, um, negative in a way that would be bad or really trying to "fix things" as we've talked about. Does anybody disagree or did I miss anything? Oh, Laurel spent some time summarizing things and pulling them together, I thought, and then going on from there.

Diane's comments allowed the group to reflect on the character and quality of its interaction, especially the value and appropriateness of their criticisms to Audrey. During the brief discussion that followed, Audrey was able to digest their advice by reflecting on how it had helped her understand the effects of her writing on readers. In her final revision she had stopped talking vaguely about "helping students identify their role as learner"; her objectives were concrete and specific; and she recognized that she understood better what she was talking about. In fact, in her self-evaluation for the course, Audrey wrote,

> This was the first class I had taken in which I was blatantly told that I was not concrete enough. It hurt at first. But after some time and more maturity, I feel that I have really begun wading through this problem that I have. I would never have volunteered to have any paper of mine evaluated if I hadn't been forced to see that my thoughts are merely theoretical regurgitated jargon.

Because the group had been able to make appropriate and genuinely useful responses to Audrey's proposal, the peer revision session was a powerfully convincing experience for all the members. The readers were surprised and encouraged by their ability to give meaningful feedback; Audrey was pleased if somewhat taken aback by the consistency of her peers' reactions with her teacher's previous observations about her writing. That consistency seemed to give Audrey the motivation and insight to confront the problem.

This revision session reveals perhaps the most important feature of peer collaboration. The group's work with Audrey's proposal gave the writing an actuality beyond the requirements of the course itself. In some respects this actuality derives from the applied nature of a methods course and the common interests of the students—but not entirely. Too often education majors regard their coursework as a series of meaningless obstacles that retard their professional preparation. But by having collaborative opportunities to develop and test their ideas about teaching, these students were able to see their assignment as a legitimate prelude to actual teaching.

Much the same can be said about the impact of peer interaction in other courses, whether they are courses in writing, about writing, or about anything else. Peer group interaction helps students bridge the gap between the "unreality" they often find in school and the vital and interesting realities that surround them out of school. Writing, then, becomes a significant activity both within the group and for purposes beyond the group.

7

Starting a Peer-Centered Writing Class

Despite the advantages of understanding writing as a process, the concept is still uncertain, particularly when applied to response groups. On the positive side, our broader perspective on writing as a process allows us to look beyond compositions to composing. We seek to guide and develop students' thinking and writing as these activities are taking place. The process approach lets us balance our interest in correct and worthwhile products with equal concern for the exploratory aspects of composing: the translation of thoughts, impressions, and feelings into language and the weighing of possibilities for developing and organizing those ideas for a particular audience. Response groups allow students to focus on these processes explicitly and incrementally.

But the concept of process also presents some unusual difficulties for teaching. We don't fully understand many basic issues in the "processing" of thought and language, such as how writers generate meaning, test it, reject it, or modify it in the course of writing. Unless we consider teaching writing much like the process of coaching someone in a complicated activity like hitting a forehand drive in tennis, we probably think about teaching and evaluating writing in terms of "things" produced. The coaching analogy suggests that you look at parts (or things) in terms of the whole movement, which is then refined and perfected as a whole. The product approach pushes us in the other direction—the whole is seen in terms of the parts. Even in so-called process-centered writing classes, students can easily mistake parts for wholes, or means for ends, if the process is presented as a lockstep series of stages with highly structured activities for each stage rather than as the messy, recursive process it really is.

Thus the minute we try to simplify writing, we easily distort it, turning it into something other than it actually is. We have Plato's problem of the cave all over again: try as we will, we don't expose students to writing but to some shadowy approximation of its pieces.

In this chapter I want to develop some practical distinctions between process and product and to show how a peer-centered writing class helps students move effectively from process to product. I'll take you through the first days of my own writing classes to show you one way to get a peer-centered class under way and keep it going. To explain why I approach writing as I do, I'll examine the process through the lens of psychotherapy, a perspective I have found to be extraordinarily useful for illustrating how the use of response groups sustains an in-process approach to writing.

Getting Started

A process-centered writing class begins as a community. Students need to feel part of a common venture, one in which their individual growth comes from their work with others, and their contributions make others' growth possible. Here, Lisa relates her discovery of the reciprocity of a peer-centered writing class:

> Unlike my other classes where I go to class, take notes, and then I'm left on my own, this writing class provided major group discussions and peer help. We functioned as a class, not as individuals. We got involved with the work of others instead of only focusing on our own work.

Classes like this work contrary to most students' experience because the emphasis is on what happens during class as much as what happens as a result of it. Teachers need to establish such classes from the very beginning, before students can slip into more familiar, passive roles.

My most successful writing classes have begun by giving students a clear understanding of how the class will work—not just by talking about it but by doing it. With first-term freshmen, for example, I use the first class to talk not just about the writing class but about how it fits into the larger purposes of a college education. Together we do some quick free writing on any of a variety of topics: why people attend college, why people write, what successful people are like. (These sorts of topics work equally well with secondary school students, especially those in major transitional years such as seventh, ninth, or tenth grades, or for college prep or AP students needing to define the goals of their English course.) By sharing the writing within the very first meeting (summarizing it, referring to it as notes, or reading it outright, which is usually what I do with mine), students immediately see that in this class, writing is something other than a private transaction between teacher and students. Moreover, they see me using my own writing to record and generate ideas and then how others' writing can add to, modify, or even contradict their own ideas. Thus the class begins by using writing as an aid to discovering and sharing ideas.

I choose a topic that I feel strongly about for that first day's discussion, one I believe will have continuing relevance for me and the class throughout the term. Any topic will do, so long as it is genuine enough and not something students perceive as just a way of filling time on the first day before the real work begins. The underlying message of this first discussion should be that we do genuine things here, not facsimiles of writing or discussing.

The next experience with writing adds to this message. The second day I ask students to choose a partner to interview, making sure they work with someone they don't already know. Their task is to use the interview as a basis for a short written sketch that will show the rest of the class something distinctive about that person. Younger students can benefit from a short list of suggested questions, but not much instruction should go into how to do the interview or what the finished sketch should look like. In fact, my goal is to make writing the sketch a natural outcome of the interview and an exercise in decision-making. The sketches are turned in the next day and by the end of the first week, "published" as a classroom handout with each entry identified by author and subject.

If I'm teaching only a single writing class, I reproduce the handout myself, letting it serve as a sort of gift to the class. Secondary teachers, with several classes and many students, might set up an *ad hoc* publication committee responsible for the typing, paste-up, and duplication. The committee may choose to illustrate the booklet or design a cover, but fast publication is most important for this activity because it serves the much-needed purpose of helping the class form itself into a community.

No reading for the rest of the term is consumed as avidly as this one. The introductions are a powerful way to let students experience having their writing read simply for what it says to others. More subtly, though, the activity reinforces in a non-threatening way the message that writing in this class is shared and that a large measure of responsibility for its quality lies with the students. Further, it inevitably puts readers in the role of deciding which sketches work well and which don't, of beginning to identify the characteristics of strong and weak writing, and of seeing, usually for the first time, where their writing stands in relation to others'.

Making this activity succeed requires delicacy. I've damaged the process by asking the class to discuss and analyze these writing samples. Looking back, I've recognized the jarring contradiction I created by telling students it was necessary and safe to write according to their own judgment and then showing them it wasn't. Instead of their sketches standing as a service to the classroom community, they became "specimens" for public scrutiny. I've since learned that rather than focusing on the sketches themselves, a short discussion of how students composed them helps to maintain the emphasis on process and provides inroads to the real questions of how writers generate texts. Important issues in the discussion concern how a writer decides what to focus on, the difficulties or tradeoffs in this decision, the relationship of the interview to the sketch itself, what various writers might like to do to revise the sketch.

These activities usually take up the first two days. They are designed to help students begin to form themselves into a community. Students need to get to know one another quickly; they need to feel that their own achievements in the course will depend on what they give to their peers and receive from them; and they need to begin to feel safe to try what may be some radically new classroom roles. Such a class runs contrary to what is familiar to most students, so it works best when established at the very beginning of the term, as a firm expectation for that particular class.

After the First Days

With the next activities I continue to help students develop their abilities to become real participants in the community we are creating. The initial readings and writings reinforce one another. I usually begin with an essay about writing, such as Donald Hall's "On Writing Well." Hall's description of writing gives the class some further insights into their own attitudes and approaches to writing. But discussing the essay as a class also maintains the emphasis on group sharing. I'm especially careful to prepare the class for these early assignments. For the first reading I write up specific discussion questions in advance. I list any terms they need to know to understand the essay fully. And I elicit students' observations about how their own writing evolves. While none of these are novel techniques, their timing is important because, done early, they establish ongoing procedures, standards, and expectations.

On the day we discuss the essay, I begin with a short freewrite, asking students to jot down their reactions to it, e.g., the most striking idea they encountered, what they remember most clearly, or what question they would ask the author if he or she were in class with us. This ensures that everyone can participate, that no one will have to grope for something to say.

At about the same time, I introduce the first writing assignment. I use a data-based assignment, for which I provide all the "data" the writer may use. I take the class through a process of data analysis, especially so they see how to use specific details to support the inferences they draw from it. In addition to the example on pages 88 and 89 on women in the labor force, such assignments might include other sets of statistics or, for younger students, a chart, a map, a table, or a fact sheet. My foremost criterion for choosing data for these assignments is coherence, that they express a single main idea, even though individual writers may perceive or address it in various ways.

In data-based assignments, everyone starts from the same knowledge base and from essentially the same controlling idea. This may seem like an assignment that contradicts the premises of a collaborative, process-oriented

FIGURE 1

Median Income Comparisons of Full-Time Workers
by Educational Attainment, 1976
(persons 25 years and over)

Years of school completed	Median income		Income gap in dollars	Women's income as a percent of men's	Percent men's income exceeded women's
	Women	Men			
Elementary school:					
Less than 8 years	$ 5,644	$ 8,991	$ 3,347	62.8	59.3
8 years	6,433	11,312	4,879	56.9	75.8
High School:					
1 to 3 years	6,800	12,301	5,501	55.3	80.9
4 years	8,377	14,295	5,918	58.6	70.6
College:					
1 to 3 years	9,475	15,514	6,039	61.1	63.7
4 years or more	12,109	19, 338	7,229	62.6	59.7

Source: Department of Commerce, Bureau of the Census.

Comparisons of Median Earnings
of Full-Time Workers by Sex
(persons 14 years and over)

Year	Median earnings		Earnings gap in dollars	Women's earnings as a percent of men's	Percent men's earnings exceeded women's	Earnings gap in constant 1967 dollars
	Women	Men				
1960	$3,293	$ 5,117	$2,124	60.8	64.5	$2,394
1965	3,823	6,375	2,552	60.0	66.8	2,700
1970	5,323	8,966	3,643	59.4	68.4	3,133
1971	5,593	9,399	3,806	59.5	68.0	3,136
1972	5,903	10,202	4,299	57.9	72.8	3,435
1973	6,335	11,186	4,851	56.6	76.5	3,649
1974	6,772	11,835	5,063	57.2	74.8	3,433
1975	7,504	12,758	5,254	58.8	70.0	3,264
1976	8,099	13,455	5,356	60.2	66.1	3,114

NOTE: For 1970–76, data include wage and salary income earnings from self-employment; for 1960 and 1965, data include wage and salary income only. Source: Department of Commerce, Bureau of the Census.

SOURCE: *Information Please Almanac*, 1979.

Characteristics of Households with Female Heads

Characteristics	1977	Income bracket	Number of households, 1976
All households	74,142,000	Household income of	
Number with female head	18,238,000	female head	
Percent of all households	24.6	Under $2,000	1,605,000
Persons per household	2.0	$2,000 to $3,999	4,826,000
Under 18 years	10,630,000	$4,000 to $5,999	3,023,000
Percentage under 18 years	29.7	$6,000 to $7,999	2,143,000
18 years and over	25,287,000	$8,000 to $9,999	1,779,000
Percentage 18 years and over	70.3	$10,000 to $14,999	2,746,000
Marital status of female head		$15,000 to $24,999	1,642,000
Married, husband absent	2,351,000	$25,000 to $49,999	438,000
Widowed	8,367,000	$50,000 and over	31,000
Divorced	3,964,000		
Single	3,556,000	Median income	$5,762

Source: Department of Commerce, Bureau of the Census.

Median Incomes of Full-Time Women Workers
(persons 14 years and over)

Major occupation group	1976 income	As percent of men's income
Professional and technical workers	$11,081	68
Nonfarm managers and administrators	10,177	59
Clerical workers	8,138	64
Sales workers	6,350	44
Operatives (including transport)	6,696	57
Service workers (except private household)	5,969	59

Source: Department of Labor, Women's Bureau.

Earnings Distribution of Full-Time Workers, by Sex, 1976
(persons 14 years and over)

Earnings group	Number (in thousands)		Distribution (percent)		Likelihood of a woman rather than a man to be in each earnings group (percent)[1]
	Women	Men	Women	Men	
Less than $3,000	704	1,137	3.9	3.0	1.3
$3,000 to $4,999	1,887	1,136	10.4	3.0	3.5
$5,000 to $6,999	4,201	2,515	23.2	6.7	3.5
$7,000 to $9,999	5,716	5,702	31.6	14.9	3.1
$10,000 to $14,999	4,259	11,671	23.6	30.6	.8
$15,000 and over	1,305	16,022	7.2	42.0	.2
Total with earnings	18,073	38,184	100.0	100.0	1.0

1. Figures obtained by dividing percentages for women by percentages for men. Source: Department of Commerce, Bureau of the Census.

class. Actually, if they're treated as a microcosm of the writing process, data-based assignments, much like sentence-combining exercises, give students an initial exposure to low-risk writing. Such assignments provide writers a chance to build confidence in their writing while introducing them to response groups in a relatively controlled, non-threatening way. Since the content of the writing isn't really theirs, students have less invested in it than in, say, a personal narrative. They find their work relatively easy to talk about, while differences of interpretation and understanding are readily apparent. Furthermore, such assignments turn out to be more challenging than they look, so students get caught up in the complexities of drawing legitimate inferences and in the details of deciding on sub-topics and choosing appropriate examples. Most important, with a common data base, students find it relatively easy to see what works and what doesn't in each others' writing. Thus, they begin to develop necessary reading skills for in-process writing and to articulate standards for good work. These outcomes are much more elusive for students writing on varied topics, in varied modes, for varied audiences. Although they ultimately need to be able to respond to a variety of writing, I have found that they can't do so without more controlled experiences first.

This assignment takes up parts of four classes. On the first day I introduce the assignment and emphasize its function as a microcosm of the writing process, and thus as a prelude to later assignments. I use a similar assignment as a dry run, something for us to talk through as a class. In this pre-writing phase, I cluster students into groups of four or five to talk about the data and decide what main idea they see. They write that idea, as a group, in a single sentence. We then share their sentences by having the recorder for each group write that group's offering on the board. Next is an analysis of the sentences for accuracy and rhetorical power. Finally, we identify the sentence we think works best and why. We talk about how they would put the rest of the paragraph together, and then I use an overhead projector to show several examples of completed paragraphs on this assignment. (Two responses to Women in the Labor Force written by students in a basic writing class are reproduced below. Although both show a reasonably accurate understanding of the data, they differ markedly in their degree of organization and readability.) Seeing multiple write-ups of the same data introduces the idea of variation among responses and gives students a chance to talk about someone's work from a previous term before they discuss their own. This helps students begin to develop a vocabulary for talking about the writing and gives me a chance to model descriptive and analytic ways to talk about a piece of writing rather than simply making blanket judgments about it.

WOMEN IN THE LABOR FORCE

Although the number of women in the labor force has been increasing, their job opportunities and wages have not kept pace with men's.

In 1978, 40,974 million women were employed. This is only a slight gain over 1975 figures of 38,414 million. However, when you look at the percentage of women in the total labor force, they comprise a substantial number. In 1978, figures show women to hold 41.6% of the jobs. While women's numbers in the labor force are high, their wages are not. In 1960, the median earnings for a woman was $3,293. Sixteen years later, in 1976, their median income had only risen to $8,099. Men's income between these years rose substantially more. Between 1960 and 1976, their median income rose from $5,417 to $13,455. Why do women earn so much less than men? One reason could be the stereotype jobs that they hold. In 1978, 34.8% of the women working were employed as clerical workers, while only 6.2% were managers or administrators. This is not a very good percentage compared to the number of women in the labor force. Equally frustrating, is the fact that in 1976, only 7.2% of the women employed made over $15,000, while 42.0% of the men in 1976 made over $15,000. I can only hope that women in the future will have the opportunity to earn higher incomes and achieve the satisfaction that an important job can achieve.

[UNTITLED]

Although women make up 41.6% of the labor force, they are being discriminated against because their pay is significantly lower than what men earn. Salary prejudice towards women is found in administrators, clerical workers, technical laborers, and all other major occupation groups. Men's salaries in 1960 exceeded the female's wage by 64.5%, rising still higher to 66.1% in 1976. The median income of women who graduated from high school stands at $8,373 while for men it goes up 70.6% to $14,295, this differential decreases only to 59.7% for females having four or more years of college. Distribution of pay by gender shows women earning $15,000 or more per year reaches a mere 7.2% and men in this percentile increases almost six times to 42%. Median income for households with females as the breadwinner earns approximately three hundred dollars less than the poverty level of $6,000. These government statistics show a disturbingly high amount of wage discrimination against this large group of employed women.

Next I hand out the actual assignment and arrange students into groups of three for a short discussion of the overall patterns they see. As I eavesdrop on each group, I try to pick up common elements of discussion, especially problems in understanding the assignment or the data. If there is sufficient puzzlement, I interrupt the class to clarify the problem or find ways to help them clarify it.

Overnight, students write a draft. The next day we talk about how they approached the writing and what difficulties they encountered. There are usually a few students who can't come up with a topic sentence or others who found they couldn't resist writing an editorial without regard for the data. This discussion gives the class an awareness of variations in their responses and thus prepares them for sharing the drafts in response groups.

To structure and direct the response group discussion, I prepare a worksheet that raises questions and requires some preliminary writing as well as note taking on the discussion:

DRAFT WORKSHOP

1. What specific questions or problems would you like your group to help you with?

2. List the major recommendations that members of your group have made.

3. Identify for yourself the next steps you need to follow to revise your draft.

Next day, the process repeats, with students reviewing each other's revisions. I provide another revision guide (see below), this time to direct students to consider more specific questions concerning the logic of their writing, the legitimacy of their conclusions, and their adherence to structural and rhetorical conventions of the paragraph. The revision guide offers not just criteria but suggestions on how to discover and apply them to this piece of writing. Again, students conclude with a few minutes to make notes summarizing their discussion and reminding themselves what they'll do for the finished piece.

QUESTIONS FOR REVISION WORKSHOP

1. Does the introduction clearly and adequately set up the rest of the essay? To determine this, read only the introduction and jot down the expectations it sets up for you, the reader. Continue reading to see whether your expectations

have been sustained. If not, should the introduction or the body of the essay be changed? What would you suggest?

2. Does the data support *everything* you say? Have you avoided sweeping generalizations (about the causes of wage and salary inequities, for example) that are not directly related to your data base? Look particularly at the relationship between the introduction and the rest of the paragraph.

3. Do the examples you have used seem adequately representative or have you stretched an example to "prove" your case? Do you have enough examples to support and explain the trends you see?

4. If you have more than one paragraph, describe the logic behind the individual paragraphs. Are the reasons clear for dividing the essay into the present paragraphs or would another arrangement be better?

5. Describe the ordering principles that seem to underlie the draft. Is your explanation consistent with the writer's? If not, where does the mismatch occur?

6. Does the draft include transitional devices to help you, the reader, see where the ideas are headed and why? What suggestions can you make?

7. Describe the voice you hear in each paper. Is there a real voice and personality behind the language of the draft or does one draft in your group sound pretty much like another? What needs to be done to individualize each one?

NOTES

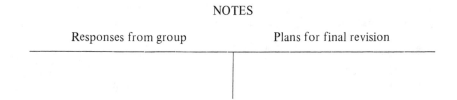

Responses from group	Plans for final revision

On the fourth day, when the paper is due, students exchange papers with a partner for final proofreading. I do this with every final paper during the term. It helps to reinforce the difference between drafts and completed writing and achieves some of the benefits of classroom publishing, even if the paper is read by only one other student. It brings the composing process to completion not just for the teacher, but for the students who have watched each other's work evolve.

The procedure I've outlined for the data-based assignment carries students through all phases of response group interaction: generating ideas, reviewing drafts, revising, editing, and polishing. The assignment results in papers that are relatively successful. And the process helps students gain confidence in their potential as writers and recognize the value of the give and take of response groups. In fact, beginnings like this help to establish necessary relationships between process and product. They forestall premature decisions and half-baked ideas and help to promote open-ended thinking in a collaborative context. To fully implement such classes, however, teachers need a clear sense of how what I'll call process-thinking differs from product-thinking, and how easily process can succumb to product. A process-centered writing class is more than an approach; it's a philosophy about how people learn and interact with one another. To help teachers sustain such a writing class, I want to explore these distinctions between process and product in more detail, using findings from psychotherapy as a way to understanding process in the writing class.

Product or Process: Fixity or Flux

Products are easy to define: they have definite beginnings and endings. They are easy to evaluate because they hold still long enough to be examined. Processes are by nature relational and contextual, in flux and constantly changing. Products satisfy our urge for constancy, predictability, closure. Processes, however, are perhaps truer to the total context of experience no matter how impossible they are to pin down. Defining the nature of process has been one of Carl Rogers' central concerns specifically in psychotherapy but more generally in education. Throughout his career, Rogers has emphasized that the key to changes in human behavior is in working with the here-and-now of people interacting with others. His discoveries about the therapeutic process have much to tell us about the composing process, especially the attitudes conducive to writing and how these are achieved through interaction.

In defining the process of change in therapy, Rogers has tried to characterize the ways in which clients come to participate in the actual moment of therapy rather than past or future events outside it.[1] He sees the change as a shift in what is essentially product-directed to process-directed thinking, from rigidity to flexibility, from closure to openness. This shift is as vital for writers as it is for people in therapy. At the one extreme, clients fail to recognize and examine their own preconceptions. They perceive things stereotypically. They resist alternative points of view because they believe theirs to be objectively true. Their thinking about problems, people, or events is generalized and abstract, often judgmental. Further, they are interested in outcomes but resist engaging in the kind of reflection and self-examination that would make the desired outcomes possible. As a result, they fail to attend to their own experience and their own role in "creating" the world they live in.

This is the dilemma of the unsuccessful or inexperienced writer. Such writers find little satisfaction in thinking through their ideas; they are primarily concerned with completing the assignment. They place little value in the details and arguments that support a conclusion because they regard writing not as an act of discovery but as an assertion of privately held truths or beliefs. Why examine or debate ideas or even recognize the possibility of alternatives once the first impulses are recorded? One's own point of view is sufficient if not absolute. Missing, then, is the willingness to engage in the *process* of writing: to examine ideas, situations, or alternatives; to hypothesize; to discover and weigh possibilities, because all these activities interfere with the outcome—a finished product.

At the other extreme, Rogers found that therapy helps clients become more flexible and fluid in their thinking. The characteristics of their thought processes are also those of effective writers: they are less "structure-bound" in their perceptions, more able to formulate ideas tentatively and willing to hold them loosely enough to test and reformulate them. Their experience is consequently fresher and more immediate, their language more detailed and metaphorical to capture nuances of meaning. Literally, their discourse is more "meaning-full" because they attend to a wider field of experience and are more actively in pursuit of the connections and relationships that make meaning. Most of all, they recognize the importance and distinctiveness of what therapists call the here-and-now (what people are actually experiencing) as the necessary forerunner to the future. In other words, effective writers have a quality of awareness of both self and others that is missing in more rigid thinking—an awareness not just of outcomes or conclusions but of the distinctive ways in which they arrived at these conclusions and might convey them to others. This reflexive, self-analytic quality of thought seems crucial among those writers who have shifted from perceiving writing as a set of results to valuing writing as a process. Peer-centered writing classes provide the environment in which this type of thinking can occur.

Another student's reflections on what she learned in a peer-centered class suggest just this sort of change, not just in her interactions with others but in her own thinking:

> I've learned that it's not bad to disagree with someone's point of view. So every time I'm reading an editorial or hearing some strong opinions from my friends, I argue with them—even if I agree with their opinion. I like to look at "other sides of the story" and try to understand it.

Therapy and Writing Classes—Essential Similarities and Differences

Therapy and writing instruction aren't the same, of course. But despite their differences, they do share a rhetorical foundation. Both require the ability to engage in learning processes that cultivate self-awareness on one hand and interpersonal awareness on the other. Members of a peer-centered writing class, like clients in therapy, need to develop flexibility and fluidity in thinking, freshness in dealing with experience, awareness of nuance and detail before reaching closure. How, though, are such characteristics achieved?

In therapy a person learns to solve problems by discussing them with someone else—talks to discover, articulate, and test alternative perceptions or problems and solutions. As a learning process, therapy helps people perceive and express increasingly fine discriminations in experience by sharing and revising their perceptions with another. Much the same is true of collaborative learning. Both result in finer discrimination in thought and perception. Equally important, however, is the process: one learns to discriminate by discriminating, by being in situations that elicit increasingly fine distinctions. In the best sense, this shaping of experience also describes the process of writing. Rather than simply voicing what we already know or believe, we use language to forge connections between ideas, to organize experience, to hypothesize and test and revise. Writing, as Donald Murray observes, ". . . is the process of discovery through language . . . of exploration of what we know and what we feel about what we know through language . . . the process of using language to learn about our world, to evaluate what we learn about our world, to communicate what we learn about our world."[2] The element common to both modes of making sense—therapy as well as writing—is talking.

Learning or Having Learned—the Crucial Distinction

The therapist's role as "audience" allows a client to experience problems "in vivo": to feel them with the intensity these problems evoke in real life. Paradoxically, therapy also allows a person to examine those problems from a more neutral perspective to understand and explain them. Both perspectives, the experiential and the analytic, are necessary. Yet experiencing needs to precede explaining much as in writing and scientific experimentation collecting data must precede analysis. Eugene Gendlin, in *Experiencing and the Creation of Meaning*, argues that only by first experiencing can people find answers to questions about their behavior. Experiencing, like describing and recording in writing, is specific and concrete. It occurs prior to the logical, explanatory aspects of thinking and learning.

In therapy, what accounts for change is, essentially, talking to the therapist. Gendlin explains it this way:

> alone [the client] can think about the same things, yet remain as he is. . . . My sense of you, the listener, affects my experiencing as I speak, and your response partly determines my experience a moment later. What occurs to me, and how I live as we speak and interact, is vitally affected by every word and motion you make, and by every facial expression and attitude you show.[3]

Thus, therapy is essentially a rhetorical situation—not in the narrow sense of clients' simply delivering then cleaning up a preconceived message but in the larger sense of making meaning by seeing it through the double perspective of themselves and someone else. The point is that in the act of talking we learn about ourselves, discover new ideas, and reach new and potentially risky conclusions that, if alone, we might very well avoid. Gendlin makes a distinction here that is crucial in distinguishing product from process. "Change in thinking" he says, "does not occur *as a result* of talking, it occurs rather *as* one talks" (p. 38).

This assertion helps to confirm our assumptions about writing: the response group is more than a sounding board for thoughts one already holds or, in writing, a final constraint on subject matter. Ideally, in writing as in therapy, we don't decide what to say then modify it to make it palatable for one or another audience. Rather, audiences help us generate and shape subject matter throughout the thinking/composing process. In the classroom, the ongoing confrontation with peers allows student writers to engage in this larger rhetorical process. When writers hear their ideas in the presence of an audience, they understand themselves differently. They hear their writing as the audience hears it because, as one writer discovered in her group, writers can project themselves, for the moment, into an audience role. Sometimes, the more critical they assume their audience to be, the more critically they can examine their own writing. However, in writing instruction as in therapy, the initial task is to overcome the defensiveness and self-protectiveness that can inhibit self-criticism in a group situation. The task of overcoming these constraints is as much the writing teacher's as it is the therapist's.

For Gendlin and Rogers, therapy is a reasonably "pure" form of learning through interaction; they believe that many of the elements of therapy are possible and desirable in other learning situations. Using what we know from therapy about effective interaction, the writing teacher must help students draw on and expand resources they already have to improve their interaction with—and consequently to better their learning with—their peers. To create such a context for writing, teachers need to alter some familiar expectations about teaching and learning. Similarly, students need to shift from passive reliance on teachers to greater autonomy and self-reliance, from doubt about the validity of their peers' contributions to belief that collaborative efforts are as fruitful as isolated ones. Underlying these shifts is something still more basic: the recognition that learning comes not solely as a *result* of one's experience but *with* one's experience. This shift, from product to process, reflects the importance of managing classroom interactions so a community of writers can flourish.

Maintaining a Process-Centered Writing Class

The distinctions I have developed between process and product should suggest that managing a collaborative writing class has as much to do with adjusting our own frame of mind as teachers as it does with what we teach. Response groups are continually new, no matter how long we have been using them, because the dynamics of any one class are so impossible to predict. Running such a class goes beyond specific practices to more subtle questions about the teacher's presence—questions of how to approach a response group, how to be both a member and a teacher, how to get a floundering group back on course.

The most successful classes are those in which students see themselves as participants in an ongoing experiment aimed at making the process work, and teachers should genuinely enlist students' suggestions and feedback. They are usually intrigued by the prospect of participating in something experimental, and an experimental approach on the teacher's part reinforces the class identity as a collaborative community.

The day-to-day implications of viewing the class experimentally are significant. In a true experiment, discovering the optimal conditions and verifying their effects are essential components. In other words, understanding the process of the experiment is as important as achieving the outcome. Based on the experimenter's observations and the participants' reports, conditions sometimes need to be changed. Indeed, the likelihood of change is the only constant. In writing classes, the teacher carefully observes students' interactions and routinely asks for information about how group members are doing. Sometimes it's useful to query an individual response group about its progress; sometimes a single student, either before or after class; and sometimes the class as a whole through learning log entries or freewrites.

Equally important from an experimental point of view, a group's failure to use its time well needs to be viewed less as a matter of goofing off and more as a sign that the students don't know how to proceed. The worst class I ever taught was a fall term freshman class in which, by some quirk of the university computer, almost half the members had attended the same small, private high school. As in many high school classes, the students exerted tremendous pressure on each other not to achieve. Instead of helping them find ways to understand and ultimately to get beyond this impasse, I tried to threaten, cajole, and punish them into doing things my way. Instead I got only more resistance. In the end, a problem like this can deteriorate into a standoff. Each time a teacher unduly pressures a resistant and unproductive group to do better, both sides become increasingly defensive and intractable. Eventually the atmosphere of the whole class turns sour.

I've since learned to maintain a constructive sense of humor and not to get impatient or defensive when a group isn't doing what I think they are capable of. I either describe the problem I see them having and ask them to talk about why, or I take a more direct approach, join the group, and let them know I'm going to model a more constructive way to handle the problem. Before leaving, I turn to someone else in the group to see if they can carry on.

Thus, the teacher's most effective stance in maintaining collaborative writing classes is to confront group behavior openly, to anticipate the problems students are likely to have, and to recognize them as a natural part of the process. Most of all, teachers shouldn't be embarrassed or defensive when calling attention to students' performance, but should couch their criticism in the context of continued encouragement, understanding, and growth. The difficulties for teachers of this sort of intervention are not different from the difficulties of being a response group participant. Like your students, you can feel embarrassed, self-conscious, or uncomfortable. This similarity shouldn't be lost on either teachers or students; in fact it's useful for teachers to recognize and acknowledge that the tension they feel about describing or intervening in students' behavior is no different from the tensions students themselves feel when we ask them to talk constructively about each other's behavior—whether in group participation or writing.

Students' reflections on their own growth in response groups shows something of their gradual development, especially as they overcome the uncertainties and fears of the early weeks:

> At first I hated these response groups because I was afraid to let people know what I thought. I learned not to be afraid of telling somebody what you think of their paper. I learned that people actually appreciate your comments and suggestions, and that I also found other people's comments and suggestions were helpful to me. I learned to look at it as constructive criticism.

Focusing again on what makes response groups initially frightening, another student writes:

> In our response groups I found it increasingly easier to give my opinion on other people's writing. This is mostly due to the fact that I know how much someone else's input helped me with my own writing. At the beginning of the quarter, it was awfully hard to give criticisms about someone else's writing because you were not exactly sure what would help the most and also because these same people would be criticizing your writing. Say what you will, most of the fear is of the criticisms you would receive in return.

Underlying both of these comments is evidence of the eventual shift to process-thinking. These students seem open to new perspectives on their work and eager to revise when they receive ideas that seem worthwhile. Since I don't grade individual pieces of writing, my students seem to revise more because they want to, less because they have to. Equally important, they have come to appreciate the reciprocity of response groups in recognizing that the benefits they derive depend on their own contributions.

Starting and maintaining a peer-centered writing class requires patience, openness, and confidence in the process. When they work well, such classes give students the confidence and freshness of thought they need to write well. The following letter is just one example of the power of peer response. There are three drafts. The first was submitted to the teacher and returned for revision. The second draft is longer but virtually unchanged, retaining all the problems in tone and perspective that make the first draft confusing and ineffective. This draft, submitted to a fellow student, also includes his marginal comments. He diagnoses the problems rather accurately and gives her the encouragement she needs to unleash herself from simply tinkering with the old problems and to radically re-think the letter. Although the third draft still has some shortcomings, most readers agree that the writer has broken through a lot of stereotypic thinking and trite language to discover what and how she really wants to write.

ORIGINAL

Dear Ross,

I could write this letter within the bounds that I should but that would be pretty dull. Instead, I will use a new program I started for myself, it's called honesty training. I'm going to tell you exactly what I think of you.

Some kind of teacher you are, making fun of people in our past. Take George Washington for instance. You jested about him just because he had wooden teeth. You even joked about James Buchanan because he was a little "chubby". I mean really a respected history teacher like yourself having no respect for the founding fathers of our country.

It's just unbelievable that an A.P. History teacher would read silly-nonsense children's stories to a class of twenty teenagers. It's even more unbelievable that just because you wrote them we were supposed to like them no matter how ridiculous. On the same scale a teacher who would sit down and play chess or have contests with the Rubik's cube with his students! A fantasy you might say, wrong again, because you did those things.

It was beyond my wildest dreams that I would get a teacher such as you. A teacher I could learn from without *discuss)* him "teaching" in the traditional sense of the profession. A man who would things with me and the class such as our views of the attempted assassination of President Reagan and the Pope, as well as the flight of the space shuttle Columbia. You even went so far as to discuss other possible ways of running our country. That to me is a teacher who wishes to open invidual minds of his students to all the knowledge the world holds.

The facts you taught me may eventually fade from my mind but I will always remember the good times we had as a class. I find your methods of teaching to be against the traditions of teaching as you are a person against the traditional teacher. I realize now how invaluable your method of teaching will be in my future education. I have no way to thank you enough.

Sincerely yours,

REVISION ONE

learning fun & fascinating

Dear Ross,

Now that I have graduated from Granger and you can't *tease me* ~~cause me any problems~~. I have decided to tell you exactly what I think of you.

Some kind of teacher you are, making fun of people in our past. Take George Washington, for instance. You jested about him just because he had wooden teeth. You even joked about James Buchanan because he was a little "chubby". I mean really, a respected history teacher like yourself teaching us things like that about our founding fathers. I always thought teachers were supposed to teach us to respect our founding fathers because they're on a level around God or at least saints *← seemingly Godlike*

Transition into different topic areas (defined topic areas) *↑↓ Tie in topic sentence relating that he was genuine, shares accomplishments.*

It's just unbelievable to me that an A.P. History teacher would read silly nonsense children's stories in

a class of twenty teen-agers. (It's even more unbelievable
that just because you wrote and illustrated them we were
supposed to like them. No matter how ridiculous they were
we were still were supposed to like them.) I have never
known a teacher to share his personal accomplishments with
his students. Although I must admit that many of my other
teachers have had egos as big as yours.

Compact between one sentence

Break down to sentences look at key words for real subject meaning

On the same scale a teacher who would sit down and play
chess or have contests with the Rubik's cube with his
students, amazing! A fantasy you might say, wrong! You
did those things and we really enjoyed it.

It was beyond my wildest dreams that I would get a
teacher such as you. A teacher I could learn from without
him "teaching" in the traditional sense. A man who would
discuss things with me and the class such as our views on
the attempted assassinations of President Reagan and the
Pope, (as well as the flight of the space shuttle Columbia.)
You even went so far as to discuss other possible ways of
running our country. It was especially inspiring to me
that we could have these discussions about current events,
going outside of the classroom. That to me is a teacher
who wishes to open the individual minds of his students to
all the knowledge the world holds. In all honesty I have
never had a teacher who attempted and succeeded in freeing
his students' minds instead of restraining them.

Example

Good

Good

The facts you taught me may eventually fade from my
mind but I will always remember the good times we had as a
class. Particularly our discussions on current events.
They made me feel like a real person instead of "just a
kid" because I could express my opinions and somebody listened and cared.

Good to include summary

Good Point

Again look at key words - shorten sentence or make 2 sentences

I find your methods of teaching to be against the traditions of teaching as you are a person against the traditional
teacher. I realize now how invaluable your method of teaching
will be in my future education and my life. I have no way
to thank you enough.

get out thesaurus

Sincerely yours,

Restate basic characteristics that make him a good teacher

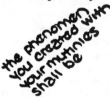

the phenomenon you created with your mutinies shall be

Be yourself - organization - It's not traditional structure - It's a matter of keeping in mind what you want to say - on track - don't forget originality - above all, don't take the whole damn thing too seriously.

REVISION TWO

Dear Ross:
    Now that. I have graduated from Granger and you 'can't
tease me. I have decided to tell you exactly what I think
of you.
    You're something else! I would have to say you are the
best teacher I have ever had. I always thought teachers
were supposed to be authoritarian figures that command respect. You are not that way, you deserve respect. You are
a very unique and genuine person. There are two things
imparticular that I can vividly remember. One is the great
chess games we used to have and the contests with the Rubik's
cube. The cube contests were great even if you did get a
little violent when you didn't win. The other thing I remember is the stories you used to read to us. Those amusing
children's stories you wrote and illustrated were certainly
entertaining. I do recall though that we were supposed to
like them if we like our grades. (Ha! Ha!) I have never
known a teacher who can be so close to his students that
he can share his personal accomplishments with them. Although, I must admit, many teachers I have known have had
egos as big as yours.
    Last year I though I was going to die of boredom. But,
super-humorous hero, you, disguised as a mild-mannered
teacher, snatched me from the jaws of death. You made
learning history fun and fascinating. You brought the
people of the past alive and made them human instead of so
distant. I remember one day that we talked about George
Washington. You told us what you thought he would have
done if he got a sliver from his wooden teeth. We laughed
so hard we cried. It was truly absurd yet it made me realize
that he was human instead of some deity, as I have been
taught in the past. You employed the dry facts (which we
already knew) as kindling and applied your humor like a
match to start a fire that warmed our minds into visualizing
the past.
    Not only are you a genuine, humorous human, you are
very easy to relate to. I recall on our free days we had
some definitely engrossing discussions. We discussed our
views of the attempted assassinations of President Reagan
and the Pope. We watched the landing of the space shuttle
Columbia and talked about what the flight would mean in the
future. I even remember one day our "discussion" got rather
spicy. We were talking about possible alternatives to the
present form of electing officials. All of us had a different
idea to take the place of the college of electorates. If we
used any of them we could hand Russia our country on a silver
platter. But everybody thought they were right. What a day
that was! These discussions were inspiring to me because we
were going outside of the classroom yet still speaking about
history, history in the making. The discussions were very
special to me for a different reason. They made me feel
like a real person instead of "just a kid". I could express
my opinions and somebody <u>listened</u> and <u>cared</u>.
    You are an easy-going, real and humorous person
which goes against the grain of a traditional authoritarian, reserved teacher. Your methods of teaching go
against the traditions of teaching. The combination of
these two mutinies formed an atmosphere that opened our
minds to all the knowledge the world holds. An atmosphere that I have never experienced before. This pheno-
menonal atmosphere you created with your mutinies
against tradition shall be a feather in my cap throughout my education and my life. I have no words that
can express my gratitude.

Notes

1.   Carl R. Rogers, *On Becoming a Person: A Therapist's View of Psychotherapy* (Boston: Houghton Mifflin, 1961), p. 131.

2.   Donald Murray, "Teach Writing as a Process, Not Product," in *Rhetoric and Composition: A Sourcebook for Teachers,* Richard Graves, ed. (Rochelle Park, New Jersey: Hayden Book Co., 1976), pp. 79–80.

3.   Eugene Gendlin, *Experiencing and the Creation of Meaning: A Philosophical Approach to the Subjective* (New York: Free Press of Glencoe, 1962), p. 15.

8

Developing
Reading Strategies
for Sharing Writing

The use of student writing as sources of reading provides a way to continue reading development beyond elementary school, where formal reading instruction usually stops. Such writing, as it evolves from drafts to finished product, challenges us to read actively, critically, and constructively. More vividly than professional works, peer texts in varying stages of development show how much both reading and writing involve making meaning, both privately and in collaboration with other readers. By treating the reading of student writing as a constructive, developmental process, I'm asserting its place within the larger framework of meaning generated through writing and group interaction. As students are confronted by ever more challenging intellectual demands, their capacity to read as well as to write and interact in groups must also continue to grow.

Prediction is a common denominator for reading, writing, and working in groups, all three of which are in some senses simply different forms of the process of making meaning with language. The leadership functions in a collaborative group hinge on prediction. Group members need to anticipate where discussion needs to go and plan how to get there. Similarly, writing necessitates prediction: predicting where an idea is heading, how it will affect an audience, and how an audience will affect it.

Reading well also demands prediction, but prediction is impossible unless readers are interacting with a text. Illustrating the necessity of such interaction, Marilyn Sternglass identifies three conditions that enable readers to make sense of what they read:

1. that readers have some conceptual basis for relating the readings to their own experience; in other words, they must have a frame of reference so they can relate new information to that which they already possess;

2. some purpose for reading the materials must be established;
3. readers should be prepared to make some predictions about what they will find in the readings so that they have some investment in the reading experience.[1]

While what I'll call lower orders of reading (reading words and sentences) are clearly predictive processes by nature, higher order reading (understanding meaning, implications, assumptions, nuances, and so on) seems to require continued emphasis on making predictions to achieve understanding. (Recall the discussion in Chapter 3 of the differences between real and ideal readers.) In this respect, reading a text depends in large part on reading its context. Such a context includes both a reader's prior knowledge, values, and expectations along with some guesswork about the writer's intentions and how well they are being expressed. This description of the reading context suggests an important parallel with the group context, which depends so heavily on those recurrent, subterranean themes that influence the group's more overt behavior. Though more loosely, these contexts also parallel the writing context, with the structural and rhetorical features that give purpose and coherence to the separate details of a text. Considered from the standpoint of prediction, reading, writing, and sharing writing are all of a piece. My suggestions in this chapter offer ways of firming up these connections by treating reading as a process of interaction between reader and text and among readers. One student's reflections on his experience with response groups emphasizes how he learned to read his own and others' writing more developmentally, always discussing writing and revising on the basis of predictions about the audience:

> When I think of response groups, the first thing that comes into my mind is "How does that affect the reader?" That thought was the most helpful for me in my writing. When I took the reader's side, many things in reading someone's paper jumped out at me. It made it easier to solve problems.

Implications of Reader-Response Criticism

Studies in reader-response criticism have shown the extent to which readers impose their own meanings on literary texts. Norman Holland's work, for example, explores reading from a psychoanalytic point of view. In *Poems in Persons* and *Five Readers Reading* he traces the consistency of specific readers' accounts (we would now call them protocols) of reading various works of literature.[2] David Bleich, in *Readings and Feelings*, makes pedagogical sense of these forays into readers' minds. His method for literary study places literature in the context of individual and communal values, based on the thesis that "reading can produce new understanding of oneself—not just a moral here and a message there, but a genuinely new conception of one's values and tastes as well as one's prejudices and learning difficulties." [3]

Bleich's rationale echoes that of many learning theories, and certainly reiterates a running theme of this book. Learning, whether through reading or direct experience, becomes palpable when it becomes personal, and it becomes personal when we reflect on it, talk about it, or write about it. Bleich notes, "just as one has to be motivated to learn to read, one also has to be motivated to think about what one has read" (4). Reflecting on what one has read is clearly not limited to literary readings. Any text becomes meaningful when readers comprehend how intimately their own values are related to the meaning that emerges from reading. Thus, the reader-response movement in literary criticism has a great deal to tell us about helping students read a wide variety of texts—literary and non-literary, student and professional.

Free Writing on Reading

A first step in helping students read peer texts constructively is to help them gain access to their reading experience. For this goal, the reading free writes described in Chapter 3 are as useful as teaching tools as they are for research. The reading free write asks students to observe themselves reading—to think about how they work on a text and how the text works on them. It allows them to monitor the evolution of meaning in a text and to identify sources of difficulty. It thus shifts attention from product to process by focusing not just on what the text says but on how that meaning comes into being.

By tapping the expressive function of writing, these free writes also introduce new possibilities. They help students assemble their thoughts and reactions in written form, which makes them available for class discussion and group sharing. As students explore similarities and differences among their responses, they gain insight into how meaning originates from the interplay of readers and text and how writing helps to shape meaning. Sharing free writes in a group is a relatively low-risk experience, since the writing is clearly exploratory and personal with no expectations for evaluation attached.

There are a number of variations on the reading free write. The most general approach is to have students write immediately after their reading. Ask them as they read to pay attention not just to what the text says but to how they are reading it:

What questions came to mind as your read?
What memories or associations occurred?
What seems most important? Why?
What seems least important? Why?

What expectations or preconceptions do you have? Why?

How did you respond to passages that seemed difficult to read?

How did difficult passages affect your understanding of the whole text?

These questions are less a checklist than a guide. They draw students' attention to the dynamics of reading, giving them guidance on how to monitor their reading process. By considering these dynamics through free writes, students begin to develop sensitivity to the dialectical nature of reading, whether it's a student or a professional text. They discover that the interaction of text and reader produces meaning, which is then rediscovered in varying ways by different groups of readers and which can be refined to come closer to the writer's intentions and the reader's understanding.

My students are always amazed when they make this discovery. Scott's comment is typical:

> Whenever I write something I always feel it is the best I can do. Our feedback groups helped me to see that there are always areas to improve. At first it was hard to criticize someone on their paper, but after we were over the hump, we were able to give good feedback. This helped me because I was able to see other people's viewpoints.

Free writes on reading are one way to begin to establish a spirit of inquiry into how texts mean, how readers read them, and how variations in readers' responses help individual readers understand, affirm, or modify their own responses. This spirit of inquiry is the essential foundation for sharing writing.

Writing Precis

A step beyond the free write toward more formal writing is the precis, by which I mean any written condensation of a text in which the writer presents the gist of the original, suggests something of the relationship between the thesis and major supporting ideas, whether narrative or analytic, and frames the text by explaining its context, purpose, or rationale. Some writers make sharp distinctions between summaries, abstracts, and precis (see for example, Charles Bazerman's text, *The Informed Writer*[4]), and some teachers may find it useful to teach each one separately. Since the basic processes are the same for all three forms, I make no such distinctions here and refer to them collectively as precis.

For development in both reading and group work, the precis is an invauable writing task. (In my own classes, I work on the precis within the first third of a term, after the data-based assignment described in the previous chapter and after a personal experience writing that I use to help solidify the class by sharing something of themselves in writing.) The precis builds on the reading free write in the movement from expressive to transactional writing and in the evolution from reading process to written product. For reading development, the precis helps students learn to distinguish overall purpose, to paraphrase main ideas and see their relationship to a controlling idea, and to place reading in a larger frame of reference for other readers—and for themselves. These experiences help transform the sometimes random or even meaningless threads of separate details into a coherent fabric of thought.

The precis can enhance group work by giving students a more or less common body of material to write and talk about. As in a data-based assignment, the relatively impersonal subject matter frees students to examine differences in the treatment of that subject. A common subject matter also reduces the tendency to drift into personal histories and validations of the writer, which can happen with the riskier task of sharing personal experience writing. This safer writing task allows groups to continue developing a language for responding to each other's work. Peers also become models for each other by showing differences in how each one approaches the writing and how well each succeeded.

Reading Response Guides

Moving the precis from process to product requires careful sequencing of group tasks. Initially sharing reading protocols and discussing the reading as a class opens up sources of difficulty in the reading, clarifies its purposes, and allows for readers' associations with it.

As students share their precis drafts (or their drafts of any writing project), they need guidance to help them read the draft actively, to show them ways to work with each other's texts to continue refining their ideas. The following alternatives (or variations on them) are useful:

A. Draft Free Writes

Peer readers can apply their skills in writing reading protocols to preparing free writes based on reading each other's drafts. These free writes give the writer an account of how others experience the writing. With a short piece, these writings can take the form of several sentences that summarize the gist of it, noting striking ideas, explaining sources of confusion, commenting on the overall impact of the writing. Such responses often look and sound like our own written responses to a draft when we're trying to convey how the writing affected us in order to suggest alternatives for revision. They shouldn't be mistaken, however, for the list of faults teachers write when attempting to justify a final grade.

B. Reading Notes

Peer readers can make notes as they read, either in the margin of the draft or on a separate sheet. Unlike the protocol, which is a more organized reflection on how a reader *has read* the text, reading notes attempt to capture how a reader *is reading*. Such notes should be focused on the reader's response, e.g., I'm confused, I like this; I don't know what this means; I see how this connects with your thesis; I remember that so-and-so said the same sort of thing; I got lost when you started on this topic, etc. These reading notes come close to Peter Elbow's concept of reader-based feedback, which he developed in *Writing with Power*. His list of questions for eliciting such feedback is invaluable for helping readers recognize the many responses they might give.[5] Groups may need to see models of such responses to learn what sorts of responses they themselves might make. I model my own reading and responding process by displaying my reading notes on an overhead projector. Reading with students, I've discovered, is as valuable as writing with them, when the sharing includes discussion of how meaning comes into being.

Reading notes are a variation of Ann Berthoff's "double entry notebook," in which she asks students to collect information, observations, or reflections journal-style and later, on the facing page, to write commentary about each entry.[6] The notebook is a vehicle for generating thinking about thinking. Here, as a stimulus to reading development, the reading notes involve readers in thinking about the reading process, making this double-sided perspective available to the writer as well.

C. Structural Analysis of Reading

Peer readers can analyze the structure of a draft with the following reading guide. It is especially appropriate for second and third drafts, when the material begins to take more definite shape and direction.

A Process Model for Reading and Revising

1. Read through the draft. Really read it. Understand what the author meant to say. Don't rely on one quick reading. Read it once to get a sense of the piece as a whole, again to look at details like what it says and how it is put together. Don't be too concerned with the exact words. Go underneath them to understand the ideas they represent.
2. Now take the draft apart. List what you think are the major ideas and state what seems to you to be the author's purpose. (This can be done either orally, going around the group, or in writing, during the class or prior to it.)
3. Under each major idea, note what the writer does to back it up.
4. Considering the purpose, the major ideas, and supporting information as you see them, what ideas affect you most strongly? What else might you need to know? What might you do differently? What would you like to hear more about?

5. Next, compare the outlines and comments prepared by each member of your group. See if the readers are consistent with each other in identifying the purpose, main points, and supporting information. See if their constructions are acceptable to the writer. What does the writer like *and* dislike about his or her draft? What does the writer regard as its strengths *and* weaknesses. If your group has differences of opinion, share them with the writer. Consider especially the additions and changes you were thinking about. Discuss what effects these changes might have and what the writer might do with them. (Remember, writers can't incorporate all suggestions; the idea is to use them to stimulate thoughts on specific ways to revise the draft.)

Conclude the session by making sure each writer has constructed a brief outline or list that includes the major points he or she will try to cover in revising the draft. It's important to provide a few minutes of class time for writers to compile their notes. The group's comments are still fresh in their minds then, and this interval emphasizes the importance of taking the feedback seriously and reviewing it carefully as a way of planning revisions.

This model helps students focus on the relationships between reading and revising by showing them how to read, analyze and discuss a draft. Unlike the protocol and the reading notes, this guide shifts attention from reader to text, still keeping the group revision process open-ended by emphasizing the tentative, exploratory features of a draft rather than its final form. Perhaps more important, it instructs students in how to use their time in the group session and demands a more active, collaborative role than peer readers often play. In describing, summarizing, and outlining their peers' texts, readers are more likely to conceive text-based suggestions for revisions than to appropriate the text and offer advice that is inconsistent with or unrelated to the writer's needs. Guides of this sort begin to break down students' association of peer revision with negative criticism. They maintain the in-process nature of a draft and replace evaluative responses with descriptive and speculative ones, which are the essence of prediction in reading. Finally, throughout this process, reading and writing are intimately connected. (Some additional reading response guides are included in Chapter 11.)

D. Reading Summary

Another way to help students compare responses to a draft is to ask each reader and the writer to work up a one-sentence summary of what each sees as the main point of the draft. By preparing the summaries independently, before discussion begins, response groups can compare variations not just between reader and writer, but among readers. Differences in these summaries are inevitable, and they provide a concrete basis for discussion as the group works to negotiate ways for the draft to evoke a more common response.

The outcome of this series of activities, from reading protocols through response guides and reading summaries to the precis, is ideally a text that reflects an awareness of ideas shaped and reshaped by language. The following precis, written by an average college freshman, is the product of this process, the result of much group debate about how to understand and represent what this writer believed were the most salient features of George Orwell's "Politics and the English Language" and how he might make clear the distinctions between his language and Orwell's.

Politics and the English Language

Many present day writers and politicians have become careless in expressing their ideas clearly. "Modern English is full of bad writing habits which have spread by imitation." Wiping out these bad habits is a necessary step toward "political regeneration," and can be achieved through clear thinking and clear writing.

Writing has become a jumble of vague and unskilled phrases. Many writers give rise to ideas they don't mean to express because their writing is unclear. They don't choose words for their clear meaning, but instead writing for them consists of tacking "phrases together like sections of a pre-fabricated henhouse." Orwell describes four main kinds of "pre-fabricated" words and phrases which he calls: (1) Dying Metaphors—metaphors which have lost their power and are used to save writers the trouble of inventing phrases for themselves, (2) Verbal False Limbs—verbs that have become a phrase made up of a passive verb attached to a noun or adjective, (3) Pretentious Diction—simple statements that falsely attempt to define a large subject in a few words, (4) Meaningless Words—words that don't define any topic, and fall short of making any sense.

Many writers tend to drift away from using concrete ideas. Thus it is necessary for an effective writer to devise a mental image of what he is describing before he attempts to write. He must take the time to choose the proper words to describe his topic or else vague phraseology may creep in and attempt to define his subject inaccurately. In political writing today, lies, deception and schizophrenia try to influence the opinion of the reader. An ineffective writer may sway his audience to a different point of view by not drawing a mental image of his topic. Orwell exemplifies this by describing a war scene where villages are bombarded, the inhabitants driven out into the cold, the cattle and huts machine-gunned, and the remaining people imprisoned or killed. He shows that in vague, insincere political writing this would be referred to as "pacification," or "elimination of unreliable elements."

Correct grammar and syntax are not as important as making the meaning clear if one is to re-establish correct and effective English usage. Good writers must use the fewest words necessary to cover their subjects, choose meanings that involve mental pictures and sensations, cut out pre-fabricated phrases and repetitions. Clear English language can help politically by restoring precise meaning to the obscurity of our political views today.

Russell G.

Creating Contexts for Reading

The research on reading has some additional implications for reading development, especially from the standpoint of reading peer texts. The more we know about a particular subject, the more discerningly we are able to read about it. Just as beginning teachers of writing gain confidence in their ability to make reliable comments about their students' writing only as they learn more about writing, so do beginning peer readers gain confidence in their readings and responses as they learn more about the subjects of their peers' writings. If my knowledge of both a subject area and of writing is hazy, I am distrustful of my own reactions, let alone of the feedback I might convey. For both of these reasons, students often comment—with some justification—on their reluctance to give feedback on their peers' work.

Consequently, the three variables I've been considering here—reading, writing and sharing—become less variable when they are embedded in a single topic of inquiry. In other words, a topical or thematic approach, in which there is some possibility for acquiring depth of knowledge over time, creates a context for reading and writing that is purposeful and communal. Endless thematic possibilities present themselves. I have structured classes around the theme of language, of education, of nuclear arms, and of women's issues. These contexts are flexible enough to accommodate individual differences, to stimulate debate, and to suggest a range of writing activities; yet these themes are also concrete enough to ensure coherence and the development of a common base of knowledge and informed opinion. With such contexts, group members develop their capacity to agree and disagree reasonably and to see reading and writing as the basis for intellectual development.

In "Collaborative Learning and the 'Conversation of Mankind'," Kenneth Bruffee argues that "we establish knowledge or justify belief collaboratively by challenging each other's biases and presuppositions; by negotiating collectively toward new paradigms of perception, thoughts, feelings, and expression; and by joining larger, more experienced communities of knowledgeable peers through assenting to those communities' interests, values, language, and paradigms of perception and thought."[7] The establishment of knowledge and the development and justification of belief are least likely to occur among students who live, intellectually, in suburban sprawl. They need the orderliness of a planned community—or at least of a city with a revitalized downtown.

Kristi's comments on one of her group experiences says firsthand what Bruffee is getting at theoretically. About midway through the term, I assign the class to write a letter to the author of an essay we've read, preferably a controversial one. Groups are formed on the basis of the authors to whom each student is writing. Kristi's group was writing to Aileen Pace Nilsen, author of "Sexism in English: A Feminist Point of View." Kristi writes:

> Being able to risk comparing our ideas to those of others, being able to have others correct and improve our ideas, and tinkering with new ways of writing were some goals that we felt the class should accomplish. I know that we've all gained experience with this by getting together in our revision sessions and comparing our thoughts on our papers. I feel that I gained the most experience with this from the workshops I was in when we discussed our "Sexism in English" letters. For whatever reasons, behind the bitterness, Trent's letter attacking everything that Ms. Nilsen said caused me to really defend what I had written and really think about my support for some of her claims. I feel that by being able to discuss what we'd written gave me some insight into my own paper that never would have occurred if I hadn't had the opportunity to discuss it with Trent and the other people in the group I was with.

The discussion was equally helpful to Trent. His first draft was so clouded by invective that his legitimate criticisms of the essay were obscured. The response group helped him see the difference between venting his own frustrations and channeling those frustrations into a more constructive tone. The opening paragraphs to the draft and the subsequent revision reflect a more balanced and reasoned approach. In addition to changes in tone, Trent has discovered that personalizing and specifying his response allows him to put his criticisms on firmer ground:

DRAFT

Dear Ms. Nilsen:

I am writing you in response to your essay "Sexism in English: A Feminist View." I sincerely hope to help you see my point of view, a slightly biased one perhaps, but nevertheless, an opposing one. (At the same time I hope that I can lessen the enormous chip on your shoulder.) The English Language, as well as its culture cannot be changed overnight. Many of the examples you have mentioned, are simply outdated and well on their way to a completely different meaning or connotation. Let us now come down from our ivory tower and take a realistic look at your essay.

REVISION

Dear Ms. Nilsen:

I am writing you in response to your essay "Sexism in English: A Feminist View." I hope to help you see my point of view, a slightly biased one perhaps, but nevertheless, a different one. The English Language, as well as its culture cannot be changed overnight. Many of the examples you have mentioned, are simply outdated and well on their way to a completely different meaning or connotation. The tone of your entire essay bothered me quite a bit. I finished it with a ripped feeling in my gut because I felt like you had put the blame totally on the males. All of society has made it so, not just men. That is the way the culture used to be. It is slowly changing, however, and so is our languge.

Genuine, lasting gains in reading and writing seem least likely to occur haphazardly, with students reading in one subject area or genre and writing in another, or jumping from one area to another with successive assignments. What students learn about the subject matter is ultimately less important than the formation of a community of learners around that topic. As Kristi's comments suggest, the communal nature of knowing invests the processes of reading, writing, and conversing with a life beyond itself. Thus, to develop reading strategies for sharing writing, we need to consider not just the step-by-step processes of shaping useful responses, but the larger context in which reading takes place. When the results of sustained inquiry are displayed in peer texts, the distance between peer and professional texts and the ways students read and respond to them may begin to diminish, making writing, reading, and responding to those texts a more purposeful venture.

Notes

1. Marilyn Sternglass, "Integrating Instruction in Reading, Writing, and Reasoning," in Janice Hays, et al. eds., *The Writer's Mind* (Urbana, Illinois: NCTE, 1983), p. 155.
2. Norman Holland, *Poems in Persons* (New York: Norton, 1973) and *Five Readers Reading* (New Haven: Yale University Press, 1975).
3. David Bleich, *Readings and Feelings: An Introduction to Subjective Criticism* (Urbana, Illinois: NCTE, 1975), pp. 3–4.
4. Charles Bazerman, *The Informed Writer* (Boston: Houghton Mifflin, 1981).
5. Peter Elbow, *Writing with Power* (Oxford: Oxford University Press, 1981), pp. 255–263.
6. Ann E. Berthoff, *The Making of Meaning* (Montclair, New Jersey: Boynton/ Cook, 1981), pp. 41–47.
7. Kenneth Bruffee, "Collaborative Learning and the 'Conversation of Mankind'," *College English* 46 (November 1984), p. 646.

9

Listening:
The Foundation for Sharing

Listening has long been recognized as the neglected language art. In 1953 an NCTE resolution called for equal weight in the language curriculum to be given to reading, writing, speaking, *and* listening. Yet while students spend more time listening than in any other school activity, they still seldom receive instruction in any aspect of it. Consequently, by some estimates people are likely to ignore, misunderstand, or almost immediately forget around 75 percent of what they hear.[1] Moreover, much schooling contributes to poor listening habits, especially teacher- and lecture-dominated classrooms that do not include frequent and substantive verbal interaction. If peer response groups are to succeed, students need to become aware of effective listening skills, and they need opportunities to practice and reflect on these skills as part of their group work. Becoming a better listener is essential to participating fully in a peer response group.

Good listening is reciprocal not just receptive; active not passive; responsive not silent. The best listeners combine verbal and nonverbal reactions to encourage a speaker and sustain interaction. For example, an experienced response group of four seventh graders was listening to one member read his paper on a scary incident when he was at home alone. One girl called attention to his vague use of the word *another*. Brandon, paraphrasing, responds, "So it's kind of confusing there?" Amy, following up, explains, "You don't know whether it's the window or the wind making the whistling noise." Brandon, instead of dropping the subject with a noncommittal "OK," presses: "So I should put, like, 'the wind made a whistling noise.'" Amy, satisfied, replies, "Yeah, I think that's better." For the most part, however, students listen passively. For them, listening is a way to garner information but not an activity that involves active, analytical engagement.

Carl Rogers, inspired by Wendell Johnson's 1949 article, "Do You Know How to Listen?," developed his earliest theories of client-centered therapy around the need to listen interactively. Johnson advanced two sumptions which Rogers used as a foundation for his own work in individual and group counseling, and later in education. First, skillful listeners attend to a speaker's content as well as to what Johnson called "circumstance" or the personal and environmental influences on how one internalizes messages. Otherwise, Johnson believed, listeners cannot know what the speaker's words mean *to the speaker* (my emphasis). Second, as Johnson states, a good listener "exercises the further attitude that any interpretation he may make of the speaker's words will be his own interpretation, and that he must take full responsibility for it himself."[2] Johnson concluded with two observations that should also serve as the foundation for peer response groups: good listening does not come naturally, and, more important, the good listener realizes that speakers can always be prompted to say more on a subject.

Reciprocity in Listening

Rogers' subsequent investigations of interpersonal relationships focus on the reciprocal value of listening with understanding:

> [Listening] is the most effective agent we know for altering the basic personality structure of the individual, and improving his relationships and communications with others. . . . If you really understand another person, . . . if you are willing to enter his private world and see the way life appears to him, without any attempt to make evaluative judgments, you run the risk of being changed yourself.[3]

These observations are equally pertinent to response groups in that an emphasis on listening is essential to collaborative growth in communication and understanding. Changes in the way people think and communicate happen even when listeners do no more than give speakers their full and uninterrupted attention.

Listeners' comments also focus and sustain discussion. Listeners can help to clarify meaning, highlight major ideas, recall undeveloped issues, elicit further elaboration, sustain thought, and point out inconsistencies. In this respect, the listener's role is to facilitate a free flow of ideas, to engage speakers in both generating and expressing their thoughts, and to take part in weaving a fabric of meaning. The focus of such listening is on the interactive process rather than on the presentation of a finished product. Speakers seldom express themselves completely either verbally or in writing without revising, and students of all ages need to know that. They need to learn that they can build their ideas collaboratively with the help of their listeners. When such collaborative listening occurs, students are practicing verbally the communication process we wish them to engage in throughout the composing process.

But listening benefits listeners too; the relation is truly reciprocal. The more time that passes without listeners making some sort of verbal response, the more their concentration and retention erodes. Through participation with a speaker, listeners can check their own comprehension of what is being said, reinforce their retention, and help themselves hear the actual message. Good listeners maintain eye contact, nod frequently, take notes, and ask clarifying questions or for repetition or restatement, all to sustain their focus on what they're hearing.

When people don't listen interactively, they often "hear" a very different message: what they wish, believe, or assume the speaker means. "The major barrier to mutual interpersonal communication," says Rogers, "is our very natural tendency to judge, to evaluate, to approve or disapprove, the statement of the other person, or the other group."[4] Introducing controversy too early in a response group can invite this sort of non-listening. Judgmental responses tend to replace attention and comprehension. However, when listeners concentrate on the speaker's message, they attend to details rather than settling for some vague approximation of "the main idea" which they then accept or reject. In so doing, listeners vastly increase their capacity to suspend their preconceptions and respond to what they hear, to analyze it, expand upon it, and only later to accept it, reject it, or substitute for it. In this sense, listeners become full collaborators, not merely passive sounding boards.

Impediments to Listening

For a number of reasons, students fail to learn to listen in reciprocal, interactive ways: the nature of the school curriculum, lack of opportunity to develop listening skills in teacher-dominated classrooms, and some characteristics of adolescent development itself.

The School Curriculum

First, studies of the curriculum continue to show that in all areas students spend most of their time in school learning information rather than engaging in the higher cognitive processes of applying, analyzing, and synthesizing what they know.[5] Typically teaching methods are product centered: *find the facts.* Even where there are no "facts" per se, students' conditioning is such that they are quick to reject multiple interpretations in favor of the quick single answer. I visited one class of honors ninth graders who were engaged in a small group discussion of a short story. Despite the open-ended, values-oriented nature of the questions, these otherwise bright, articulate students never proposed more than a single answer to each question, so concerned were they with answering all of them quickly, and so readily did they assume that every question had but one correct answer. The students listened not so much to what was said, but, like Carl listening to Kate's trial sentence (in Chapter 4), they simply recorded the noise that filled the aural equivalent of a fill-in-the-blanks exam. Whether intentionally or not, much schooling discourages interactive listening by minimizing any need for it.

✓ *Teacher-Dominated Classrooms*

Second, traditional classrooms tend to locate authority in the teacher—whom students perceive as having right answers. The mode of listening that results is a passive, receptive one. Furthermore, peers tend not to listen carefully to one another, partly because long association convinces them they already know each other's ideas and partly because they perceive that there is no reward for listening to someone of equal status. Thus students acquire little or no experience in the active, inquisitive aspect of listening; in fact they learn to discredit it. They assume that people either know or they don't know; facts are facts; teachers are responsible for what gets known, not students. Given these assumptions, many aspects of the peer response experience, especially listening, are not just unfamiliar but untrustworthy as well.

↙ *Adolescent Cognitive Development*

Third, and probably the most understandable, is a pervasive and over-generalized aversion to the idea of criticism. Perhaps because of the association in students' experience between criticism and bad grades, they are reluctant to receive criticism from peers, as well as to give it. This aversion seems to originate in the cognitive style characteristic of the late adolescent years. William Perry's research on college freshmen, for example, revealed that many students at what he called the "dualistic" stage of development think primarily in terms of simple but absolute dichotomies: good or bad, true or false, known or unknown.[6] Coupled implicitly with this cognitive style is a rejection of the fluid, tentative evolutionary approach to meaning in which constructive criticism plays a central role. In its place are all the characteristics of the single step, product approach.

Even when students progress from the absolutist thinking of the early, dualist period to an awareness of alternatives, they tend, as Perry discovered, to maintain the rather noncommittal attitude characteristic of the next period of development—multiplicity. Here, very little outside the unequivocal truths of the hard sciences can be known for certain; what isn't known for certain is mere opinion; and one opinion is as good as another. From this perspective, critical interaction is a waste of time in students' narcissistic assurances to each other that "I'm OK, you're OK." This relativistic attitude shows up in students' beliefs about what constitutes good writing. In an interview study of college freshmen and sophomores, including those who took advanced placement English in high school, I found that students routinely described good writing as that which is "clear." They resist any suggestion that some ideas might be better than others; so long as what you've said is "clear" and "well-organized," you've produced good writing.

Perhaps as a result of their conviction that good writing is clear writing, students almost *never* contradict another student's proposed revision and rarely challenge or disagree with the content of an essay. Instead, peer readers prefer to limit themselves to safe, familiar issues of mechanics and usage (questions that have rather definite answers), clarification of existing ideas, and, though infrequently, improvement of a paper's organization. Missing is the vast and more essential middle range of collaborative exploration and modification that interactive listening makes possible.

A peer response centered writing class, however, can begin to overcome many of these obstacles by changing the very circumstances that give rise to them. As previous student comments have shown, students are finally appreciative of the diversity of perspectives their peers have to offer. They can learn to listen purposefully, both for their own benefit and others'. They can overcome the narrow-minded reliance on grades alone as a measure of achievement. And perhaps most important, they can see how writing evolves from draft to draft, becoming not just clearer but different—and qualitatively better. Trent (interestingly, the anti-feminist young man whom Kristi referred to in the previous chapter) sums up the reciprocity of effective listening this way:

> Responding to other people's writing was new to me. I had never been given the chance to listen to someone's writing and actually tell them what I thought was good or bad. This helped my own writing immensely. Different people's ideas, insights, and style suggestions are a real help.

Getting inside students' initial reluctance and modeling alternatives seem to initiate change. I observe students' first group experiences carefully and after the second or third meeting I introduce instruction in listening and interacting by saying something like this:

You've probably noticed that we're going to be spending a lot of time working with each other in these response groups. I think you're doing a great job so far. You seem comfortable with each other. You seem to stay pretty well on the subject. I hear some good comments. Let me try now and then to show you some even better ways to make the time you spend together useful. You need to think about what I'm going to tell you now as constructive help, just like what you're trying to give each other on your writing. Sometimes it's hard to do that and not feel or sound like you're putting somebody down, but I'm giving you this feedback in the spirit of helping us all learn to work together as well as we can.

And I proceed to make some concrete suggestions about how to listen to each other more effectively or to provide useful feedback. Before the

groups meet the next time, I remind them of what we agreed they shoul\
This approach helps keep students' attention focused both on their wr
and on learning to work productively in their response groups.

Developing Listening Skills

In an early study of listening, Ralph Nichols and Leonard Stevens conclude (rather sanguinely, perhaps) that "in most cases, awareness of aural
deficiencies is enough by itself to make people do a better listening job on
their own." [7] To begin, then, teachers can promote students' awareness of
listening just by describing what good listeners do and by helping students
discover for themselves what distinguishes good listening from bad and how
each affects both speaker and listener. One student remarked to me that he
had so taken listening for granted that he never imagined there were different
ways to do it, much less ways to do it better.

Observation and Inference

As with other aspects of learning interaction skills for response groups,
activities that develop listening complement both the goals and methods of
writing instruction. Since direct observation is one of the primary sources of
information for a writer, projects in which students observe people listening
provide opportunities for field observation that serve a genuine purpose in the
collaborative writing class. Subjects for observation vary widely: class discussions, family dialogue, discussions among friends.

Videotapes of television talk shows and interviews are also sources that
teachers can bring into the classroom for observation and analysis. PBS frequently offers relatively sophisticated group and panel discussions. At the
other extreme talk show hosts, and sometimes guests, frequently provide a
catalog of poor listening behaviors: interrupting, digressing, changing the
topic, imposing unrelated points of view, avoiding the issue, making speeches,
and so on. Similarly, television interviews such as Barbara Walters' reveal a
type of interaction that is least desirable in workshop groups: the stycho-
mythia of prepared questions and on-the-spot answers that is less conversation
than interrogation. For secondary schools, where instruction in listening is
usually required but never really taken seriously, studies of this sort meaningfully integrate listening and writing instruction.

In studying listening, students will quickly discover something of the
palpable limits of observation and the need to extend them inferentially.
Below are sample questions to guide the students' observations and shape
their interpretive abilities:

1. What do people do when they listen to one another?
2. What do people do that shows they are listening closely?

3. How do you know when they have heard and understood the message?
4. What do people do that shows they are *not* listening closely?
5. How do you know when they have *not* heard or understood the message?
6. What is good listening?
7. What is bad listening?
8. For both speaker and listener, what are the difficulties and benefits of listening well?

The questions progress from observation of physical details to inferences and conclusions based on those observations. Students should gather that good listening isn't so much observable as felt, an intensity of common thinking that goes beyond technique, and is manifest in the easy collaboration of speaker and listener.

Since listeners can listen faster than speakers can speak, good listeners use their spare time to promote better listening. The students' conclusions about good listening should, in part, parallel these researchers' discoveries:

1. The listener thinks ahead of the talker, trying to guess what the oral discourse is leading to, what conclusions will be drawn from the words spoken at the moment.
2. The listener weighs the verbal evidence used by the talker to support the points he makes.
3. Periodically the listener reviews the portion of the talk completed so far.
4. Throughout the talk, the listener "listens" between the lines in search of meaning that is not necessarily put into spoken words.[8]

In other words, good listeners listen much as good readers read, learning in the context of the discourse to make predictions about where the speaker is headed and how well she is getting there. Students should discover that good listening is part of a helping relationship, in which even seemingly adversarial comments are given in a spirit of sharing. Moreover, they should discern that many attentive listeners do so with pen in hand—that listening and writing are intimately related.

Practice

Despite Nichols and Stevens' optimism, understanding the functions of listening isn't enough to make it happen in response groups. Once students have surveyed listening in the field, they need guided activities in their groups to apply their findings to their own behavior. Such activities engage them not only in a useful analysis of some of the thought processes necessary for research and writing, they also make possible an ongoing self-assessment of the

writing group's listening behavior. To develop listening skills, students
to distinguish four dimensions of listening: *attending, reflecting, drawing*
and *connecting.*

Progression of Listening Skills

Attending → Reflecting → Drawing Out → Connecting

Attending

The most common failing of group discussion, large and small, teacher-
and student-led, is students' judgment that their peers' comments are unimportant. In *Developing Effective Classroom Groups,* Gene Stanford maintains
that with their continuous pattern of paragphrasing each student's contribution, teachers unintentionally diminish their value: "This habit of repeating
reinforces students in the habit of not listening. Why bother, when the
teacher is going to repeat everything anyway? It communicates to the students that they don't need to listen to one another, only to the teacher." [9]
Helpful as this interaction may be to teachers in reinforcing their own attention to students' comments, it robs students of the same opportunity. Moreover, since the paraphrase is generally given in clear, more precise language
than the original statement, students have even less reason to attend to their
peers, for they will get a better version from the teacher. Consequently, they
find themselves lacking the listening and interaction skills so ably practiced
by the teacher. As a result, they tend to distrust the worth of what their
peers might contribute and to doubt the value of their own observations.
What follows from this is an egocentric preoccupation with one's own ideas,
bolstered by impressive evidence that peers have nothing to add.

Focusing on attending helps students find a way out of this egocentric
trap. One exercise involves giving the group a controversial topic to discuss.
Ask one student to state his or her position and the reasons for holding it.
The next student must then summarize that person's position before explaining why and to what extent she agrees, without introducing any disagreement,
no matter how strongly she may actually oppose the positions. The next
student summarizes *that* position, then introduces his own reasons for agree-
ing. And so on around the group.

The purposes of this exercise are to structure attention to the details of
each other's comments, to find some basis for agreement, and to rule out the
more common tendency to juxtapose unrelated comments or positions. On a
more subtle level, the exercise begins to shape a cooperative attitude toward
group work while encouraging sustained discussion of a single topic.

As important as the exercise itself—or any exercise—is the group's
awareness and analysis of how the experience fits into the larger context of

group development. At the end of the exercise, the group should conduct a short evaluation session to respond to these questions:

1. What did members of your group do to show that they were paying careful attention to your contribution?
2. Did you feel that you were being heard and understood?
3. What might your group have done differently to promote better listening and understanding?

Reflecting

In addition to the non-verbal signs of attending, paraphrases of a speaker's comments are the most reliable and widely used means of ensuring attention and conveying understanding. Like its written equivalents, verbal paraphrasing helps listeners internalize what they have heard. Yet if teachers respond to virtually every student comment with a paraphrase, the common pattern of student-to-student interaction is for one student to narrate something from her experience and another to respond in kind:

A: I'm going to write about my history teacher last year who always put people down either by making fun of them or making them feel stupid.
B: Yeah, I had a teacher like that who . . .

While the intention here is to suggest the students' common experience and thus to validate both the topic and person, the resulting discussion will focus on inconsiderate teachers in general rather than the history teacher in particular, falling off into the kind of bull session students and teachers alike are skeptical about. But by paraphrasing some or all of what A said, B makes it possible for A to continue thinking about that teacher because he has metaphorically reflected back to A what he heard. The paraphrase might be limited to surface content: "You mean that this teacher embarrassed students by making fun of them and making them feel dumb."

Or the paraphrase might begin to reflect some of the implied content: "You don't feel that this is a very effective way to teach." Or "The teacher must have always looked for the worst in students."

To begin reflecting this way, students again need to observe actual conversations to see the forms in which paraphrasing occurs and to be reassured that it isn't such a weird way to talk as they might at first suspect. A number of films for use in counselor training provide excellent models of good listening; other films have been developed for training purposes in schools, businesses, and industry.[10] Just as useful is to appoint one or more students to observe a whole class discussion, count the number of paraphrases they hear, and describe their findings to the class. Alternatively, tape record a class discussion and assign a small group of students to analyze the discussion and report to the class.

Once in their response groups, students should try to paraphra‹ other's remarks as a way to promote greater depth and comprehensio... ‹..‹ student found that he could be most helpful in listening reflectively when he kept in mind the question: "What is he trying to say?" If students continue to listen and talk superficially, try these options:

1. Assign one student as observer for each small group with the same task as that in the large group—to count the frequency of paraphrases and describe what he hears or what substitutes for paraphrasing.
2. For at least part of the discussion, set the rule that each new speaker must satisfactorily paraphrase what the previous speaker said before making her comment. Although no one should construe this procedure as a model for all group discussion, it does heighten awareness of how little we understand of what others say and provides very deliberate opportunities to practice reflecting skills.

Drawing Out

The next stage of this listening continuum involves helping speakers elaborate on ideas by "drawing out." In *Reality Games,* a practical guide to improved communication, the authors describe the speaker in any discussion as the "focus." Any speaker can be the focus, but the point is that each speaker should remain so until he or she has run out of things to say about the topic. The other participants are to act as facilitators and keep the speaker talking—generating, exploring, and developing ideas.[11]

The goal of this exercise is to teach listeners to use a speaker's subtle cues to elicit more material rather than letting discussion drift aimlessly from topic to topic and speaker to speaker. Particularly when students are brainstorming topics in response groups, the focus game helps them recognize the difference between pointed and aimless discussion and gives practice in pursuing depth and detail for subsequent writing. In other words, drawing out a speaker is the oral equivalent of drawing out a topic in writing; it's a thinking skill students need to practice in a variety of modes.

There are several methods for developing listening by drawing out a speaker, all variations on this game. While reflecting through paraphrases remains integral to the process, questioning also enters in to help the speaker identify related issues, alternative points of view, additional implications, or new ideas. Whether students are initially brainstorming a topic or reviewing a draft, the same discovery questions apply. Sax and Hollander phrase the issue this way:

> Often when we talk about something, we merely reel off old ideas, old feelings, old perceptions. When we do this, there is a kind of mechanical deadness in our discourse. Our old perceptions, old ideas, old feelings no longer fit us.[12]

The role of the facilitator, or listener, is to encourage the speaker, to bring about fresh insights, in a sense to revise his or her thinking. In this respect, drawing out is an invention strategy that, like any prewriting strategy, can help the writer generate ideas. As an invention strategy, drawing out applies as much to oral discourse as it does to writing. In both cases, it is most likely to occur when the listener tries to think, see, and feel as the speaker does rather than imposing his or her own ideas and experiences or directing the discussion in a preconceived way.

Once students understand the differences between these roles and their functions, they are ready to practice. To begin, assign pairs of speakers and listeners. For younger students, it's useful to describe the listener as one of the nosiest people they can imagine, someone who wants to know *everything* connected with the speaker's topic. Give the speaker a topic to discuss (or use topics for writing assignments that group members have already chosen), and ask the listener to keep the speaker talking for five minutes. Afterward, let them critique the discussion, answering these questions:

> What did the listener do to draw you out?
> Did the listener help you to keep talking?
> Did you discover new ideas or were you saying what you already knew?
> What might each of you have done differently to improve the discussion?

After a brief analysis, set up a new topic, let the pairs switch roles, and repeat the process.

Help students understand that the roles of speaker and listener are still necessary back in their discussion groups, but that within the group, each member is at different times playing either role. For writing workshops, the student presenting a paper or a set of ideas is the speaker, while the group, as listeners, draws out the speaker/writer. When the listeners have finished, the writer needs to become the listener, in turn drawing out group members for their ideas or suggestions. The same critique questions apply at the group level. In an experienced group, these roles will shift naturally and automatically. In a beginning group, however, students need to be aware of the constraints and purposes of each role to avoid falling back into the kind of egocentric, free association described earlier.

Connecting

The most sophisticated of the listening skills is connecting. It involves a hierarchy of cognitive skills, from remembering individual contributions to seeing their similarities and differences, discerning implications, and synthesizing the results. Among the shortcomings in student interaction that Stanford and Roark describe in *Human Interaction in Education,* the tendency to make multiple, unrelated comments figures prominently. Wh... happens is something these authors call the "skyrocket phenomenon," in which "each member contributes by 'firing up a skyrocket,' that is, by introducing a new, unrelated idea for the group to marvel at."[13] When the group is instead able to make connections among the many comments, it shifts, in essence, from sounding board to switch board, imposing order and coherence on the mass of material the group has generated and connecting the messages of senders and receivers. If a group discussion is to be truly useful, participants need to derive from it a sense of connectedness and direction so they can come away from the discussion with some useful ideas and ways to implement them.

To develop the ability to make connections, students need to make summarizing a natural part of their discussion. A summary brings together and condenses ideas, involving skills in selection and organization. It also provides one last chance to clarify or modify members' perceptions of what was said. Equally important, members' awareness that someone will offer a summary helps them keep the discussion on track; the fact of a summary reinforces the idea that the discussion should be purposeful.

Connecting skills need to be shaped slowly and deliberately. If developing writers fail in their *writing* to perceive and draw connections between one idea and another, their oral discourse suffers the same problem. In both cases, the tendency simply to list ideas or to rely on simplistic connections such as spatial or chronological ordering suggests that the analysis and synthesis involved in connecting are not yet well developed thinking skills. Consequently, in large group discussions, teachers need to resist the temptation to do all the connecting for students and instead to provide opportunities for them to see and express these links.

There are several possibilities for developing connecting skills in discussion. First, in class discussions when one comment bears a relationship to something said earlier, ask the students to explain the connection. Rewarding them for doing so, especially for volunteering to provide connections, encourages students to recognize these responses as they occur naturally. Second, assemble lists of the various kinds of connections: amplifying or expanding; identifying similarities or differences; qualifying, clarifying; defining. During large group discussions ask for specific types of connections or label them as they emerge spontaneously (e.g., "What you're doing now is giving a good, concrete example of the idea Sharon was talking about a few minutes ago."). Finally, seize upon points in discussion when a summary would be appropriate, and ask class members to provide it. These practices not only help shape students' connecting abilities; they also support the need to listen actively, since students will become more directly accountable for what has been said.

In small groups, where students are more autonomous, the need for connecting must remain a conscious issue. One option is to rotate the job of summarizing, breaking discussion time into intervals of increasing length: a summary after three minutes, after five minutes, and so on. Another option is to chart the kinds of connections identified in class on a tally sheet (see Chapter 11 for an example) and use an observer in each group to record the frequency of each type. Third, use critique or de-briefing sessions, either in large or small groups, so students can analyze the effects of connecting, both on the quality of listening and interaction as well as on the group's productivity.

Finally, shift the focus of the connections from the verbal interaction to the papers themselves as students begin to work with drafts. Peter Elbow's approach to summarizing is especially useful here: first, members should summarize the main points of a paper as they remember them; then summarize in a single sentence; then in a single word from the writing; finally in a single word not in the writing and different from its language.[14] This approach takes students through a progression from content to response, blending practice in memory, condensation, perception of structure, paraphrase, and evaluation—an application to writing of the progression of listening skills just discussed.

The paper below is the outcome of several response group sessions in which students were trying to listen for undeveloped themes in their narratives about a "turning point." Paul's initial draft was a well written ("clear") but basically stale narrative of his decision not to pursue a college football scholarship. His group attempted to draw out more of his feelings of conflict over that decision to help him find a more universal meaning in the experience, something that would take the essay beyond simply chronology. The group's careful listening and probing led to this more thoughtful revision:

DISPOSABLE HEROES

I feel so left out. I never thought I'd really miss it. Here I am, standing in the middle of a little league football team with a notebook full of plays and a whistle around my neck, trying to stay involved, but it's just not the same now. Coaching football just doesn't feel the same as playing.

A couple of years ago I decided that I wanted to play college football. To help me out, my high school coach started to send some of my personal information around to all of the universities in the area, and soon my dreams seemed to be coming alive. I started getting many letters from major college athletic departments giving information about their campuses, teams, and coaches. Many letters had reply cards that I eagerly filled in and returned, hoping each time that my chances of playing college football were increasing.

During the summer before my senior year, I made a few goals for myself that would help me become a better ball player. I decided that I

was going to have to be the strongest, fastest, smartest defensive line-
man that I could be in order to impress those college coaches. Every
morning before the sun was up, I would be at school running stairs and
lifting weights until I was totally exhausted. Then, each night, I would
run about five miles more. I knew I had to be in excellent physical
condition before school started because a lot of my time would be
taken up then with studying.

As the year went on, a few schools sent some of their coaches out to
meet me and get to know me better. They were all interested in me and
they gave me tickets to some of their home games. One school in particular, Weber State College, was very serious and one of their coahces
would call me every couple of days just to keep in touch. But then it all
happened.

One night I saw a documentary on television titled "Disposable
Heroes." It was the story of ex-football players. This program opened
my eyes to many issues that I hadn't ever thought about. I had just
been picked to the All-Region team and my attitude about football was
much less than humble. I felt I was as good as the next guy and I would
be doing the school a favor by playing football for them.

But then it all changed. The program based its story on an interview
with a man who played for the Chicago Bears. He didn't look like a
football player. He was sitting in a reclining chair wearing a pair of
shorts and a tee-shirt. His knees were packed in ice to keep the constant
swelling down and his back was strapped in a brace that restricted his
movement completely. He couldn't work, so he tried to sell insurance
by phone. This man had been a football hero? But one Sunday after-
noon, he blew his knee apart in a game and was disposed of by his
team. His football career was over and practically so was his life. But
the thing that really affected me was that this man couldn't even pick
up or play with his two-year old son.

After watching this program, I didn't know whether I really wanted
to play football or not. I knew that there were many things in my life
that I enjoyed and even more things that I was looking forward to and
all of a sudden football didn't seem so important.

The next time the Weber State coach called, I told him about the
feelings that I had. I felt that football was the greatest sport that I had
ever played, but I didn't think it was for me after high school.

So here I am, in the middle of a little league team, regretting my
decision. Only time will help me realize that what I did was the right
choice.

In the progression of listening skills, students move beyond the passive
listening and halting interaction so characteristic of much group discussion.

They learn to monitor their own behavior in groups and to recognize that they are legitimately responsible for the success or failure of their discussions. Above all, they enable themselves to discern where these successes or failures lie—at the same time that they acquire skills for coping with both dimensions of the group task, the content as well as the process.

Notes

1.   Robert Bolton, *People Skills* (Englewood Cliffs, New Jersey: Prentice Hall, 1979), p. 30.

2.   Wendell Johnson, "Do You Know How to Listen?", *ETC* 7 (Autumn 1949), p. 7.

3.   Carl R. Rogers, *On Becoming a Person: A Therapist's View of Psychotherapy* (Boston: Houghton Mifflin, 1961), pp. 332–33.

4.   Rogers, p. 330.

5.   See, for example, Arthur Applebee, *Teaching English in the Secondary Schools* (Urbana, Illinois: NCTE, 1981) and D. Trachtenberg, "Student Tasks in Text Materials: What Cognitive Skills Do they Tap?," *Peabody Journal of Education* 52 (1974), pp. 54–57.

6.   William Perry, *Forms of Intellectual Development in the College Years: A Scheme* (New York: Holt, Rinehart and Winston, 1968), pp. 59–71.

7.   Ralph Nichols and Leonard Stevens, *Are You Listening?* (New York: McGraw-Hill, 1957), p. 16.

8.   Nichols and Stevens, p. 82.

9.   Gene Stanford, *Developing Effective Classroom Groups*, p. 123.

10.   "Three Approaches to Psychotherapy II, No. 1: Dr. Carl Rogers," 48 min., Psychology Films, 1981; "The Power of Listening," 26 min., CRM/McGraw-Hill Films, 1981; "Verbal Communication," 30 min. CRM/McGraw-Hill Films, 1982; as well as these older films: "Listen, Please," 10 min., BNA Communications, 1959; and "Listen Well, Learn Well," 11 min., Coronet Instructional Films, 1951.

11.   Saville Sax and Sondra Hollander, *Reality Games* (New York: Popular Library, 1972).

12.   Sax and Hollander, p. 42.

13.   Gene Stanford and Albert Roark, *Human Interaction in Education* (Boston: Allyn & Bacon, 1974), p. 108.

14.   Peter Elbow, *Writing Without Teachers* (New York: Oxford University Press, 1973), p. 86.

10

Giving Feedback

Students usually construe feedback as criticism or evaluation—always negative—or sometimes as advice, which they understand to require an expertise they don't believe they have. They also worry that they'll get as good as they gave—that harsh criticism of others' work will come back to haunt them when their own work is on the line. Terms such as *feedback* and *response* help to defuse the powerfully negative connotations of "criticism" and need to be used deliberately in defining the task of response groups. These words begin to suggest more neutral ways of responding to writing than do the destructive implications of "criticism." Habits, though, are hard to break: students readily revert to describing how they respond to one another as "criticism," however euphemistically "constructive."

Teachers too convey to students that their task is essentially a critical one. In an article otherwise supportive of the value of feedback in composition, Walter Lamberg refers to a "limiting view of feedback and of responses from readers . . . that the information or responses must be qualitative or explicitly evaluative." No matter how we seek to disguise it, feedback can still mean implicitly "judgments as to what constitutes good writing." [1] Unless the role of feedback in writing workshops is carefully explained and consistently maintained, we are asking students to do what nearly anybody would go to great lengths to avoid doing.

Despite students' reluctance to give feedback, they apparently help each other more than they realize. Research not only seems to uphold the common-sense conclusion that students receiving feedback show more improvement in writing than those who don't; it also gives the edge to peer over teacher feedback. [2] One of the most remarkable advantages of learning to *give* feedback, as my students explain it, is its impact on the student's own writing. Lisa comments, "I know for a fact that outside input on my writing helped me to see different aspects, etc. But giving input even helped me

131

ask myself my own questions regarding my work." The problem, then, is how to overcome students' aversion to the idea of feedback so they can use it to its full potential.

Understanding Feedback

To arrive at a solution, we first need a clear understanding of what feedback is and what kind we can expect students to give each other in writing workshops. In the scheme I'm presenting here, feedback completes a response continuum begun by listening (see Figure 1). The continuum is organized according to the degree of risk involved for both readers and writers. Reflecting responses are less risky than connecting responses; supporting feedback is less risky than challenging feedback.

FIGURE 1

Response Continuum

Attending	Reflecting	Drawing out	Connecting		Supporting	Challenging	Editorial
	Listening					Feedback	

Listening, as I argued in the previous chapter, is largely a writer-centered heuristic. Listening helps writers discover ideas, clarify, amplify, and connect thoughts and impressions. Although students need to use the listening skills I outlined throughout the composing process, their chief value comes into play during the exploratory phases of writing. Feedback, on the other hand, moves the writer from invention to revision with peer reviewers taking a more active role in helping writers develop their ideas and refine their expression. Although feedback, too, is essential throughout the composing process, writers can neither give it nor receive it usefully until they have learned to listen to one another.

The concept of feedback originated with cybernetics, a branch of epistemology that includes information and communication theory. In cybernetic thought, communication is not linear, from A to B, but circular and consequently interactive: from A to B back to A, and so forth. Technically, the loop that returns the communication to A is the feedback, or feedback loop. Communication theorists, perhaps a little hyperbolically,

seem generally to agree that the advancement of the feedback lc
is, in intellectual history, about as important as the Copernican
For instance, this passage from *The Pragmatics of Human Comn*
suggests that the shift in our understanding of communication fror
circular has made possible, among many other things, the current view of
writing as process:

> As long as science was concerned with the study of linear, uni-directional,
> and progressive cause-effect relationships, a number of highly impor-
> tant phenomena remained outside the immense territory conquered
> by science during the last four centuries. It may be a useful over-simpli-
> fication to state that these phenomena have their common denominator
> in the related concepts of growth and change.[3]

In other words, the concept of feedback expands the traditional linear model
of Think-Write which underlies the product approach to composition. Instead,
feedback is central to the recursive, process model of writing in which the
concepts of growth and change figure so fundamentally. Applied to writing
and discussion the model looks like this:

FIGURE 2

The Feedback Loop in Writing

Decision-making
Generating Ideas

Feedback
Self Feedback
Peer Feedback

Feedback
Self Feedback
Peer Feedback

Drafting/Revising

As this model indicates, the encouragement of feedback in writing
workshops isn't merely a useful pedagogical tool; it's fundamental to the
processing of information. Feedback signals the degree to which a writer has
conveyed information to readers rather than "noise," the undifferentiated,
chaotic backdrop against which messages stand in contrast. Communication
occurs when receivers discern what structure they think constitutes the message, then loop their guesses back to the writer for confirmation. Put another
way, they make predictions about what the message might be and ask the
sender to confirm their predictions. The interaction between sender and

receiver, writer and reader, comprises feedback. Feedback allows the clarification of messages—a re-shaping or re-organizing of the initial structure.

This isn't just another, more complicated way of saying that writers need to anticipate readers' needs; it's a way to emphasize two related matters: (1) the centrality of feedback to the writing process—the *whole* process; and (2) the inherent flaw of much writing instruction, especially classes where students write only for the teacher and only to prove that they know what they're charged with knowing, e.g., the causes of the Civil War or what photosynthesis is. In these instances, students write without the precise intentionality that informs structure and organization for various audiences. Without definite intention, any number of structures will serve the writer, as will the most general feedback.

Without having a reason to write what one intends—to someone who will benefit from reading it—a writer is satisfied with virtually any forthcoming feedback. In fact, feedback has the unfortunate power in these situations to mold the writer's intentions to match the expectations or desires of the readers. The fuzzier the intention, the less exact the feedback. Comments like "That's good," or "That's interesting" suffice for both reader and writer. Reflecting on her unsatisfactory experience with response groups in high school, one senior wrote, "In high school the response groups weren't constructive. You would always hear, 'Yeah, I like it,' or 'That's good,' and that would be the end of it. I guess everyone was concerned with hurting feelings."

The ideal at the invention and early draft stage is for the writer to have some loose idea of what to say and how to organize it but to be interested in working with the group to discover collaboratively better meanings and more definite arrangements. The problem is to teach young writers how to give and receive meaningful, constructive feedback.

Inasmuch as receiving feedback poses relative degrees of risk, I've divided it into three types: supporting feedback, challenging feedback, and editorial feedback. The distinctions are both emotional and developmental. Supporting feedback focuses on writers' attitudes toward their drafts and engages group members in making descriptive, reinforcing commentary. Challenging feedback comes closer to the great bugaboo, criticism, because it calls for reader responses that at least imply evaluation. Challenging feedback becomes useful only when the group has established secure working relationships and has learned some preliminary analytical skills and how to convey responses effectively. Editorial feedback completes the continuum—and the revision process—by exposing texts to the group's scrutiny for correctness and stylistic effectiveness. Coming at the end of the response continuum, editorial feedback is the most explicitly evaluative of the three types (even though it also deals with mechanics). But by the time the group has developed a comfortable working climate, students should be able to view editorial feedback as constructive rather than assaultive, collaborative rather than evaluative.

Seeing the evolution in a student's work from draft to revision is useful in understanding the effects of feedback. Ron's first draft of his research on body language is halting, stilted, and confusing. In talking about the paper, he realized he had been making assumptions about the need to maintain an objective, formal tone and had been trying unsuccessfully to incorporate those conventions into his work. The revision shows that Ron gained confidence in his own voice. The language is more vivid, the explanations clearer, the organization more apparent. Through the feedback he received on his work, Ron was able to step back from his draft to reconsider it, in the process clarifying his ideas and finding more effective ways to express them.

PERSONAL SPACE INVASIONS
(Draft)

Until recently, few Americans were aware of the importance of body language and its influence on others. Personal space is one of the areas of interest in studying body language. It's presence can be felt in areas which we communicate to others both verbally and nonverbally. The use of personal space is evident in the way we communicate socially, publically, with different ethnic groups and also in sex roles to name a few. Violation of personal space affects the way we act in all of these environments.

You may wonder, what is personal space. It may be defined as the area individuals maintain around themselves in which others cannot intrude. Many people think of it as a bubble of space that surrounds us. But bubbles can be popped, so I would like to think of it as an electrical field. It can have an attraction for bodies as well as repulsion. This force can decrease with distance and at the same time it isn't circular like a bubble but can be three dimensional. Being noncircular, it can extend much farther in front and shift in size to the rear.

Permeability is the way we react to the intrusions of our personal space. The degree of discomfort experienced is proportional to the extent of intrusion into ones' personal space.[1] Experimenting with personal space, one day at Church I sat by a girl who I have become friends with, but nothing more. As I talked to her I slowly moved closer to her. She would then move away, closer to the friend she was with. I again moved over and this time I put my arm on the bench so it was around her. Within five minutes she was leaning on her friend with her knees pointed toward her. Even though we are friends, it was obvious that I had invaded her personal space.

Something else I tried was moving in on a friend as we talked. I would take a step closer and could feel the uneasiness in him as we kept talking. Then without realizing it until I told him what I was doing, he would take a step backward.

Even though I have tried to define personal space and permeability, scientists have had problems trying to get realistic measurements of discomfort levels because they are not the same for all people. Experiments have been done where the subjects are approached and they tell the experimentor when they feel discomfort. We cannot assume that it is true in real life situations.

There are several different categories in which personal space shows its effects. In business transactions with a clerk or a repairman, for example, we use a social distance. We use it in social gatherings or in a more dominating effect as with a teacher to pupil or a boss to a secretary. Social distance is based on the notion that "it is not the density per se, but the proximity of others that is important. This measure is the sum of the reciprocals of the distance from any one individual to each of the other individuals in the setting."[2]

Violating some of these social distances led me to agree with the research done. Studying in the library gave me some opportunities to test this idea. I noticed that some people would spread their things all over a table, a nonverbal clue not to invade their space. So I sat myself down next to them and slid their things over to make room for myself. This seemed to confuse them at first, then one person kept giving me dirty looks and another person just got up and moved.

Another place that I tested social distance was in elevators. There seems to be an unspoken rule that you must stand as far away as you can from all others, never talk, and just stare at the floors as you move. When I got on the elevator, I picked a person and stood close to them. Then I stared right at them. Most of the people I tried this on ignored me as best they could.

School sets up a good example of a more dominating social distance. I have observed that most classes are very formal with a teacher behind a table and sometimes using a podium, giving me a feeling of distance and authority. The answers to questions I asked in these situations were given with a feeling of authority by the professor. Then, when I tried approaching him after class and penetrated his barrier to ask a question, he became more friendly and personable.

Worchel and Teddlie, in experimenting with different social conditions claimed that "interaction distance and not density per se is the spatial variable that is related to crowding."[3] It is in social gatherings and crowding that we find that the nearest people are the main cause of the crowding that we feel. Even anticipating that potential nearness of others can affect us.

Sex is another area in which personal space has been studied. It has been hard to research because the overall results are too inconsistent to support any one idea or theory of its given effects. Studying male to male, female to female or male to female is difficult in itself, but we must also consider physical and biological sex differences that cause many imbalances in interacting. "It is not just biological sex per se that directly determines where one stands . . . (but also) complex cognitive and social processes that incorporate information on sex into ones' status, plans, fears, urges, needs, objectives, and behavioural style."[4]

We do know for the most part, that women tolerate smaller distances between themselves and others than men do. The same distances make men uncomfortable. Of course, intimate male-female pairs tend to keep the smallest physical distance. Violating personal space in sex does not always bring out discomfort; other feelings can be caused by its effects. Many theories have come about to help explain its effects but I will only use a few major ones for examples.

The attribution approach is "altering interpersonal space that creates nonspecific arousal."[5] For a positive relationship the approach will tend to be closer. A negative approach will cause reactions to compensate for a closer approach. For example, to reduce a relationship you use methods to cool down the relationship by using nonverbal communication. So feelings can either be positive or negative as personal space is invaded.

Although the attribution theory is the most accepted, a lot of attention has been given to the equilibrium theory. It proposes that "several dimensions (eye contact, distance, topic intimacy, smiling) are governed by approach and avoidance forces." For example, standing too close produces anxiety from potential touching and standing too far away makes conversation difficult. It suggests that an equilibrium is maintained by compensating and changing for any imbalance that might arise. People who cannot together reach an equilibirum will most likely quit a relationship rather than fight an imbalance. The way we change in approach or avoidance forces will either help to enhance or decay the relationship as personal space is infringed upon.[6]

The investigation of cultural space shows that Latin American, Mediterranean, and Arabian people are "contact cultures" and American and European are "non-contact cultures."[7] You could expect Italian, French, Russian, Spanish, Latin American or Middle Eastern to like close personal contact, while the English, Scandinavian, Swiss and German avoid close personal contact.

I have a Mexican friend that I work and play basketball with who helped me to understand this observation. I noticed that as we talked he was always closer to me than I was comfortable with and he touched a lot. I watched in his relations to other American workers as well. He would be close to them and they would be uncomfortable and usually back up.

Playing basketball, it was also evident to me and others that he seemed to play much closer and more physically than the rest, who were Americans. This would bring an uneasiness because of expected distances in talking and playing than we are accustomed to.

In researching personal space and its effects, I have found it hard to get exact real life measures but there are measures that generally show personal space does exist. For example, measuring sex differences is difficult because of the many possibilities. We can see, however, that spatial violations produce flight, blocking, discomfort, and negative impressions along with the other body language we use can aid in the reaction we get when intruding on peoples personal space.

(Editor's note: This and the revised version were fully footnoted.)

SPACE INVASIONS
(Revision)

Until recently, few American were aware of the importance of body language and its influence on others. For example, what effects do your posture, gestures, facial expressions, costume, the way you walk, even your treatment of time and space have on others? Space, or personal space is evident in the way we communicate socially with people, publicly with teachers and speakers, in different sex roles and also in different ethnic groups. The best way to see the effects that personal space has on others is to notice the reactions of people as their space is violated.

You may wonder, what personal space is. Many people think of it as an area we maintain around ourselves, which we would feel uncomfortable if others intrude. You may have heard of it as a bubble of space that surrounds you. But I would like to think of it as an electrical field that can be like a magnet. If you have an attraction for someone you can be pulled closer together, but it you dislike or are unfamiliar with a person, you can feel a repulsion towards them. Just as a magnet, we can be drawn to or repelled from people who invade our personal space.

Being like an electrical field, it also means that it doesn't necessarily have to be round like a bubble, but can be a different shape. You probably use more space in front of you than you do in the rear.[1]

An intrusion of our personal space usually causes discomfort or an uneasiness. Hayduk tells us that "the degree of discomfort experienced is proportional to the extent of the intrusion into one's personal space."[2] Experimenting with personal space, one day at church I sat by a girl who is a friend (but nothing more). As I talked to her, I slowly moved closer. She, in turn, would move away from me and closer to her friend she was sitting by. I again moved over and this time I put my arm on the bench behind her so it was around her. Within five minutes, she was leaning on her friend with her knees pointed towards her. Even though we are friends, it was obvious that I had invaded her personal space.

Something else I tried was moving in on a friend as we talked. I would take a step closer and could feel the uneasiness in him as we kept talking. Then without realizing it, until I told him what I was doing, he would take a step backwards.

These two reactions by my friends show that personal space does exist and also the uneasiness and discomfort that it can cause if it is violated. They both had the same basic reactions even though they were of different sexes, the violation of their personal space caused them to move until they felt comfortable again.

There are several ways in which we use our personal space. One of them is a social space or social distance, which is about four to seven feet. It is the space we maintain in social gatherings. Our space is not affected by the general mass of people, but the people that we are associating with or those who most closely surround us. Knowles also made this observation when he said that "it is not the density per se, but the proximity of others that is important."[3]

In testing this idea, I tried violating some social distances and came to agree with Knowles. My first place was studying in the library. I noticed that some people would spread their things all over a table, a nonverbal clue not to invade their space. So I sat myself down next to them and slid their things over, if they were in my way. This seemed to confuse them at first. One person gave me dirty looks and another person just got up and moved.

Another place that I tested social distance was in an elevator. There seems to be an unspoken rule that you must stand as far away as you can from all others, never talk, and just stare at the numbers of the floors as you move. When I got on the elevator, I picked a person and stood next to him. Then I stared right at him. I could tell that most of the people that I tried this on were uncomfortable and would turn away from me and ignore me as best they could.

The examples here show that when social distance is violated, not everyone is affected, just those who were close to me and felt discomfort as their space was intruded upon. So whether we are standing next to someone in an elevator, seated next to someone in the library or in some other social setting, people have their certain space that they like to keep. Don't be surprised if you are in one of these situations and you find yourself closer to someone than they would prefer and they give you a look as if to say, "Don't you think you are a little close?" or maybe they will just pick up and leave.

With social distance, there comes a more formal or public distance used by teachers in classrooms or speakers at public gatherings. This distance extends to 25 feet and beyond. School sets up a good example of a more dominating public distance. I have observed that most classes are very formal with a teacher behind a table and at times using a podium, giving a feeling of distance and authority. The answers to questions I asked in these situations were given with a feeling of authority by the professor. Then, when I tried approaching him after class and penetrated his barrier to ask a question, he became more friendly and personable.

The effects of public distance are close to that of social distance, because in interacting with people, it is the distance of the people closest to us or those to whom we are talking that influence the use of our space. Worche and Teddlie said, "It is the distance in which we interact with people that gives us a crowded feeling, not everyone is involved."[3] For example, if you were teaching or speaking, you would be more aware of the people who are closer to you than to those who are farther away.

The personal space we use with a member of the opposite sex is another area that has been studied. For the most part, women tolerate smaller distances between themselves and others than men do. The same distances make men uncomfortable because they generally need more space. Of course, intimate male-female pairs tend to keep the smallest physical distance.

Violating personal space between the sexes does not always bring out discomfort, if a couple like each other, they will tend to stay closer to one another. However, if one person in a couple doesn't want to be close, that person will generally send out signals to let you know.[4] Lets say that you try to hold a girl's hand and the girl doesn't want to. If you grab her hand, she may either pull it away or just let you hold it and not make any response when you touch her hand, she tolerates it. Situations here can be either positive or negative. We also use a space when communicating with a friend of the opposite sex. The distance you will use depends on the relationship. However, standing too close to your friend can make her feel uncomfortable, while standing too far might make it hard to understand each other.[5]

In violating the personal space of a member of the opposite sex, we should remember that the person might want to be close to you, or maybe that person will want some distance. We should be aware of the other person and look for clues that can tell you what that person might want.

Our personal space is not only affected socially, publicly or in sex roles, but also between cultural differences. The investigation of cultural space shows that Latin American, Mediterranean, and Arabian people are "contact cultures," and American and European are "non-contact cultures."[6]

I have a Mexican friend that I work and play basketball with who helped me to understand this observation. I noticed that as we talked, he was always closer to me than I was comfortable with and he touched a lot. I watched in his relations to other American workers as well. He would be close to them and they would be uncomfortable and usually back up.

Playing basketball, it was also evident to me and others that he seemed to play much closer and more physically than the rest, who were Americans. This would bring an uneasiness because of expected distances in talking and playing than we are accustomed to.

Personal space is a part of body language that can tell us a great deal about relationships between people. Most people in every culture have a fairly strong sense of how close they will allow other people to come. In most situations, in which we deal with others, requires some personal space. When that space is violated, it can cause flight, blocking, discomfort, and negative impressions, depending on how we choose to deal with the situation.

Feedback Continuum

To fulfill its supportive function, feedback must meet four criteria: the writer must ask for it; the feedback must focus on what the writer is capable of changing; it must be reinforcing; it must be empathic. These criteria are discussed more fully below.

1. Feedback is perceived as supporting when the writer solicits it.

Writers need to initiate the feedback process by asking for responses. The more precise their requests, the more specific the feedback, and hence the value of asking students to write their questions before the group meets. We know from the analyses of reader- and writer-based prose, and from the distinctions between self-expressive and transactional writing, that at some point writing and thinking move from private to public. Transactional, or reader-based, writing needn't be finished, but it must at least be ready for scrutiny. However, many students' experiences with writing in school have taught them that it's a secret communication to an omniscient teacher who will fill in gaps in meaning out of an infinite fund of knowledge. The fact that teachers usually know more about most subjects than their students to some extent supports students' perceptions of an omniscient reader. Therefore, they don't fully distinguish reader- from writer-based prose or self-expressive from transactional writing. In itself, the invitation to decide when a draft is ready for feedback affirms these distinctions among the variations of writing and makes them all acceptable forms of expression, though their contexts differ.

Having writers ask for specific feedback also lessens the likelihood that they will lose ownership of their work by needing to act on every suggestion their group makes. Early in students' experiences with groups, this is a common reaction and a source of considerable frustration. Teachers need to anticipate this and warn students away from it early on. My colleague, William Strong, recommends that we describe feedback as gifts, only some of which we like. We say thanks, use some and quietly put the others away.

For readers, the writer's invitation to give feedback is equally important. The need for harmony is among the most powerful constraints in student groups. So long as students think that giving feedback really means giving criticism, they are reluctant to do so and politely decline to enter where they've not been invited. On the other hand, when a fellow writer asks for specific feedback, students are more likely to give honest and thoughtful responses.

2. Supporting feedback focuses on what the writer can do something about.

Although the goal of the feedback process is to generate new ideas and perceptions, discussion needs to begin in safe, familiar territory. Equally important, readers and writers alike need strategies for moving from the known to the unknown. Otherwise the tendency is to assume complacently that all the writer's thinking is embodied in the draft and that the group's task is simply clarification and clean-up.

To center a workshop around issues a writer can do something about, ask writers to begin by discussing two sets of questions:

- What are the strengths of this draft (or idea)? What do you like about it? What was easy for you?
- What are the weaknesses of this draft (or idea)? What do you dislike about it? What was tough?

These questions serve two purposes. First, they remind the group of the paper's interim status, that it's an object for study and further development. Second, since writers initiate discussion with their own impressions of their writing, these questions implicitly allow writers to establish a focus and to set some initial boundaries for discussion of what they feel they can handle. Eventually, the boundaries of the discussion will expand so that everyone gets a chance to make the comments they believe are important. Thus, feedback initiated by the writer, what might be called "writer-based feedback," tends to open outward to include "reader-based feedback," the perceptions of a writer's colleagues in the group.

3. Supporting feedback is reinforcing.

Contrary to students' (and many teachers') most deep-seated convictions, reinforcing feedback produces more change and a greater motivation to learn than critical feedback. Common sense favors negative, even punitive feedback. You can't fix what's wrong until someone has pointed it out to you. Hence our strong inclination to focus on weaknesses rather than strengths. Our preference for negative feedback, though, is part of our linear, Think/Write, product heritage. The shift from product to process, however, means that feedback should function not to punish error but to encourage and guide continued thinking. Supporting feedback comes about when readers believe in the writing enough to get inside it and move around, to try on the ideas as if they were the reader's own.

Reinforcing feedback is not, as a simplistic definition might suggest, solely an ego massage for the writer (although a little bit of that never hurts). Encouraging students to make comments like "That's a good idea"; "I really like the way you said that"; "I understand exactly where you are going" opens up the dialogue and, perhaps more important, can encourage attentiveness to details in a paper. For at least the first half of a term, I require groups to identify two or three things they like in a draft—words, sentences, ideas, stylistic devices, even good spelling. I've found that I need to reiterate this requirement frequently, even to require that readers write out their positive comments, because they are too apt to jump prematurely into a critical stance. One group of seventh graders admitted that while they tended to launch right into criticism of each other's work, each one really wanted to hear about something he or she had done well. In my own classes, sessions in which we read aloud from learning logs provide me with an opportunity to model and further encourage positive and supportive comments on writing. Back in response groups, asking each group member to express, for instance, two good things about a draft, means that they have to read carefully enough to find those commendable features.

Reinforcing feedback functions cognitively as well. Like reflective listening, it conveys acceptance and understanding and establishes a common frame of reference for reader and writer. The collaborative relationship that results helps to dispel students' almost Pavlovian association of feedback and CRITICISM. Accordingly, writers tend to become more energetic in developing their ideas, especially in discovering latent possibilities in what initially seemed complete.

4. Supporting feedback is empathic.

To be reinforcing, feedback must also be empathic. Empathy is most often described as a state of being: a listener's tendency to assume another person's frame of reference, paradoxically at the same time the listener remains grounded in his or her own reality. It's also important to point out, however, that in addition to its psychological quality, empathy is both a way of thinking and expressing oneself—both essential aspects of writing and discussing writing. As a way of thinking, empathy is an immersion into another's ideas in such a way that you temporarily suspend your own point of view and try to see the world through the other person's eyes. Dendi, a college freshman, describes this process nicely: "The thing that really helped me to respond to others' writing was that I was to become the person the paper was addressed to." This involves not only taking on an alien frame of reference but also thinking it through as if it were one's own. What psychologists label "advanced accurate empathy" calls for high-level cognitive ability:

1. summarizing core material, which means discriminating between the essential and non-essential
2. picking up implications
3. identifying themes
4. isolating premises and assumptions in order to help the other person draw conclusions
5. defining alternative perspectives or interpretations.

At its highest level, empathy involves more than the non-judgmental reflections described in the previous chapter; it engages the listener in collaboratively exploring and developing ideas.[4]

At the same time, empathy also demands verbal sophistication. In his preface to *An Experiment in Empathy,* John Wilson observes, "we can only know that the world I inhabit is like the world you inhabit if we both describe it in similar terms."[5] The communication of empathy, ranging from basic description to analysis and synthesis of ideas, fulfills an important function in exploring and articulating ideas for writing. As years of research into interpersonal communication have demonstrated, empathy raises the level of exploration of a problem. In his 1980 publication, *A Way of Being,* Carl Rogers sums up this considerable body of research by asserting "that empathic people enable others to begin revealing material that they have never communicated before, in the process discovering previously unknown elements in themselves."[6]

Rogers' emphasis on revealing and communicating is significant. An empathic audience helps us organize and articulate difficult concepts as we speak—a way of hearing, revising, and even preserving our thoughts prior to getting them down on paper. From the undifferentiated noise of consciousness, such an audience helps us distinguish ideas, images, and impressions.

The evidence suggests that people can acquire empathic skills rather quickly. In practice, though, these skills are disturbingly shortlived. David Jacobs observes in his study, "Successful Empathy Training," that people don't spontaneously and naturally make the kinds of responses known to be empathic. Instead, as he points out, they "already believe that widely diverse forms of responding are subsumed under the task of being helpful empathic. These include giving advice, introducing a new perspective, evaluating motives, ... and so forth." Consequently, in much psychotherapeutic training, Jacobs continues, "the specific manner in which subjects are asked to respond so violates their own sense of what a 'good' response is that . . . they pretty much ignore the instructions."[7]

Jacobs' training program demonstrates the impact of empathic feedback. When his trainers acknowledged to trainees the alien quality of empathic responses, when the trainees clearly understood why some responses were better than others, and when they received immediate and sustained feedback on their responses (in essence, feedback on their feedback), their capacity to make such comments outside the training situation seemed to increase and endure. In short, by introducing a feedback loop and treating the trainees' problems empathically, Jacobs dramatically enhanced their learning.

Much the same thing holds for student writing. Give students a chance to get inside each other's writing not just during composing but after you have responded to it. Pair students or group them in threes. Let them read your comments and explain to each other what the comments mean. They are giving feedback on feedback this way, and they are getting inside *your* frame of reference to understand better the values and expectations you hold for their writing.Empathic people are those who can project themselves into another's experience. They understand things as the other person does, have similar emotional responses, and can communicate these responses. In short, empathy is non-egocentric. Developing it is largely a process of de-centering, to use Piaget's term. It's no coincidence, therefore, that recent research in writing development has centered on egocentricity as one of the fundamental cognitive and rhetorical obstacles for young writers to overcome, and that we look increasingly to collaborative learning to help in this de-centering process.

To understand the potential of collaborative learning for reducing egocentricity, we need to be clear about the meaning of egocentricity. It *can* mean that the individual isn't fully capable of entertaining points of view other than his own, as is the case among young children. Perhaps more important, however, the term also suggests a lack of access to other perspectives. Contrary to the implications of much developmental research, one doesn't reach a magical age at which egocentric thinking disappears forever. If students are to de-center their writing, they must have opportunities to de-center their thinking. To do so, they need to practice overcoming egocentric thought not just in writing but in all aspects of thinking and communicating.

Role Playing and Feedback

Exercises in role playing provide a powerful means for overcoming ego-centricity and developing empathy in group interaction and writing. Role playing is both cognitive and social. Cognitively, one must understand a person's attitudes, values, and motives, and be able to make predictions about that person's behavior in order to play that role. In this respect, cognitive development is an internalized process of role playing, modeling, and emulating. Socially, role playing provides a kind of "reality practice," the trying on of another's role to feel out alternatives before committing oneself. By playing the role of someone else, people can often think or say what they might not as themselves. It's sometimes safer, easier, and more useful for a reader to say, "If I were Professor X I'd be suspicious of this conclusion," than it is to say, "I think you're coming up with the wrong conclusion." Projective statements like this one are also more comfortable for a writer to hear.

To visualize the possibilities for role playing in developing the capacity for empathic feedback and non-egocentric thinking in writers and readers, consider the classic rhetorical triangle (see Figure 3). Each point in the triangle suggest a role that can be manipulated, either for writing assignments, group discussion of a paper, or both. With each manipulation comes a change in the relationship suggested by each line of the triangle: a writer's view of the subject, a writer's relationship with readers, a reader's view of the writer, or a reader's view of the subject.

As these possibilities suggest, role playing offers opportunities for de-centering thinking on several fronts—social, linguistic, psychological, and cognitive. Equally important, it reinforces the generative nature of group work and downplays the evaluative. Each role playing situation requires students to examine a topic from a new perspective and to consider the ideas that result. In the process, role playing affirms the rhetorical dimensions of writing—that one writes from various perspectives, for various reasons, and for various audiences with various needs. For instance, the roles students might play can be located along a continuum from most to least familiar, most to least personal. Role playing also extends the potential audience available for student writers, depending on the variety of roles group members become able to play. It also gives peer readers opportunities to review their peers' texts from many perspectives, which enlarges the scope of the peer audience.

Challenging Feedback

The danger of supportive feedback is that, used exclusively, it can create a laissez faire atmosphere in which anything goes. Though it is necessary for successful writing workshops, it isn't sufficient. Challenging feedback

FIGURE 3

Role Playing and the Development of Empathy

—write *as* different people
—write *for* different people
—listen to feedback as different
  people

—read and give feedback as different
  audiences
—read and give feedback as the writer
—assign a different response to each
  group member (task master, sum-
  marizer, paraphraser, re-writer, etc.)

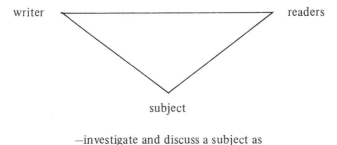

writer   readers

subject

—investigate and discuss a subject as
  different people with varying kinds
  of access to the subject and points
  of view about it
—reverse a thesis and discuss the
  results to generate or test ideas

must eventually become part of the group's interaction skills. Teachers give challenging feedback routinely. Unlike students' imitations of their behavior, however, the best teachers provide challenging feedback by asking for clarification, citing counter-examples, challenging generalizations, identifying hidden assumptions, and so on. Interestingly, none of these responses is evaluative in the condemnatory sense that students imagine. All guide students in thinking analytically about a conclusion or about the way they have arrived at it. Unfortunately, students have little chance to practice giving challenging feedback when teachers tend to assume this responsibility alone.

The process of developing skills in challenging feedback is very much like the one outlined for developing listening skills. Students should assemble an inventory of the possible ways to challenge or question an idea, then rely on this inventory as a guide in reviewing each other's work. The goal, of course, is eventually to incorporate this sort of feedback automatically into one's thinking; but at first it needs to be used quite deliberately, even mechanically, with students being guided by a checklist.

Ideally, a class or group should generate its own criteria for analyzing or questioning their work, and these criteria need to be fitted to specific writing activities. As a stimulus, however, I have adapted the following list of challenges from Louis Rath's *Values and Teaching.* [8] To make them more concrete for students to use, I offer a series of questions associated with each challenge. (See Table 1.)

TABLE 1.

An Inventory of Challenging Feedback

Type of Challenge	*Questions*
reviewing alternatives the writer considered but rejected	Why did you choose this alternative? Why did you decide against this explanation, this illustration, this thesis, etc.?
eliciting other explanations or solutions	How else might this come about? How would so-and-so solve this problem? What else might make a person behave this way?
applying a generalization to a different, sometimes more complex situation	If the situation were this way, what could happen? What interpretation would you make? What conclusion would be possible?
testing the universality of a belief or conclusion	Would/should everyone hold this view? If they did, what would happen? Does this conclusion hold in all cases? What if . . . ?
challenging point of view	Who might see this differently? How might they see it? How would their circumstances affect their interpretation?
defining a term	What does this mean?

Type of Challenge	*Questions*
citing exceptions or eliciting exceptions	When might this not work? not be appropriate? not be desirable?
examining the limitations of belief or conclusion	For whom, when might this idea not apply? Are there some circumstances under which this would not be so?
defining conditions under which a conclusion is true	What makes you believe this? Can you think of a situation when you might change your mind?
locating inconsistencies	Does this belong? Does this fit? How does all of this fit together? Is this the right/best order?
assessing the strength of counter-arguments	If you believed the opposite, what would your reasons/conclusions be? What other arguments might be raised?
checking the validity of a source of evidence	What makes you believe this source? What other sources of evidence are available?
asking for the degree of someone's certainty	What would you need to change your mind? How strongly do you believe this? Under what conditions would you put money on it?
distinguishing fact from opinion	How do you know? Is it observable? If I saw what you saw, would I come to the same conclusion? Are you making a value judgment?

For students to become comfortable asking each other questions like these, they'll need to practice either in a neutral, large group discussion or in a small group situation they can observe and analyze. Turning then to the response group, I help the class generate several challenges appropriate to that assignment and then delegate one or two sets of questions to each member. This way the questions are opened up to the whole group to discuss and resolve as they pertain to each paper.

An inventory like this gives students a set of structured criteria for providing challenging feedback. Unlike the responses students typically make in groups, challenging feedback like this depends upon a reading of the draft itself, not a response to the writer or to the vague reconstruction of the draft that peer readers often seem to create in their minds. When readers respond to the text, the danger of feedback-as-criticism is also greatly diminished, since the interpersonal worries about attacking one's peers aren't as central to the task. Finally, coming as it does after extended interaction, challenging feedback becomes less of a trial-by-fire, more of a genuinely collaborative process. Practiced this way, feedback can provide student writers with well-developed options among which to choose, not the half-baked advice or imperatives that students more readily give each other.

Editorial Feedback

Despite the emphasis on discovery and revision, the concept of a composing process nevertheless implies a beginning and an end. Thus, the response continuum I'm developing here concludes with editorial feedback—the lexical, syntactic, grammatical, and mechanical guidance that peers seem to want to give each other from the very beginning but that should be delayed until a more appropriate stage. Editorial feedback has to do with preparing, reviewing, and polishing a finished text. The role of the peer reader becomes that of copy editor, reviewing texts to improve style, correct errors, and bring the piece into conformity with established standards. Appearing at the end of the response continuum, editorial feedback shouldn't be an avoidance strategy to salve over some frightening group dynamics—as it does when student groups provide it too soon. By this time, groups have established secure working relationships, and editorial feedback can thus serve the more important function of sharpening style, logic, and diction along with more basic "objective" issues of correctness. One of the most efficient methods for incorporating editorial feedback is as follows:

Using groups of four or five members, establish four or five categories or criteria against which to review final drafts; for example, subject-verb agreement, punctuation, syntax, diction, coherence, and structure. Ask the groups to draw on member expertise by assigning a category to each person, the best person to read drafts for that element. Ask students to pass papers around the group so that each member reads each paper, penciling in corrections or comments and consulting other sources, such as handbooks and dictionaries, to resolve any uncertainties. The goal is to make the group accountable for the group's texts and to submit polished pieces teacher's review and evaluation.

When papers are finally ready to be turned in, pair students f final proofreading, teaching them how to pencil in corrections and what specific kinds of errors to look for. At first students are reluctant to make marks on clean, polished pieces, and they'll at first read only perfunctorily. But with repeated trials over successive assignments, they get better at understanding the place and necessity of a "perfected" piece of writing and probably also at sensing an ownership of their work.

This method also helps students develop a mature perspective about the teacher's final evaluation of writing by letting students see how the teacher's final function as evaluator and critic complements the students' function as collaborators. For example, the students in Brad's group (discussed in Chapter 5) learned that their responses to each other's work didn't replace the teacher's judgment. They came to accept grading as simply another type of feedback: a descriptive response designed to bring about continued improvement rather than a punitive final judgment. The seventh graders reached much the same conclusion. Said one, "At first I would write just to get good grades. But now I write because I like to."

The humane but rigorous peer review process I have described seems most likely to help students place their teacher's judgment about the merit of their writing in the context of the many descriptive and evaluative activities that have been coupled with the writing/review process all along the response continuum. In this respect, product and process are mutually reinforcing: process engenders products; once complete, one product stimulates the process of continued development.

Notes

1.   Walter Lamberg, "Self-Provided and Peer-Provided Feedback," *College Composition and Communication* 31 (February 1980), p. 64.
2.   See Daniel R. Walter and Walter J. Lamberg, "The Effects of Feedback on Writing: Research, Review and Implications," ERIC #140355.
3.   Paul Watzlawick, Janet Helmick Beavin, and Don Jackson, *The Pragmatics of Human Communication: A Study of Interactional Patterns, Pathologies, and Paradoxes* (New York: W. W. Norton, 1967), p. 30.
4.   For a fuller discussion of advanced, accurate empathy, especially its empirical basis, see Robert R. Carkhuff, *Helping and Human Relations, Vol. VI: Practice and Research* (New York: Holt, Rinehart and Winston, 1969).
5.   Samuel Natale, *An Experiment in Empathy* (Slough: National Foundation for Educational Research in England and Wales, 1972), p. 11.
6.   Carl Rogers, *A Way of Being* (Boston: Houghton Mifflin, 1980), p. 155.
7.   David Jacobs, "Successful Empathy Training." *Journal of Humanistic Psychology* 21 (February 1981), p. 40 and p. 55.
8.   Louis Raths, et al., *Values and Teaching: Working with Values in the Classroom* (Columbus, Ohio: Charles Merrill, 1966), pp. 260–261.

11

Troubleshooting:
A Miscellany of Suggestions

This chapter provides a catalog of additional group activities to serve as a troubleshooting guide for writing groups. The activities are designed to increase the group's awareness of its own behavior, to give teachers and students the skills necessary to solve group problems as they occur, and to keep groups from experiencing many of the failings outlined in earlier chapters. The activities here are intended to be suggestive, not prescriptive. With these ideas as cues, individual teachers should be able to develop activities adapted to their own students and their own environment as well as to design other techniques.

Establishing Groups

It's important to consider individual peer response groups as subsets of the larger classroom group. Without the guidance, support, and direction of the class, small groups can't develop the climate of warmth, trust, and openness they need to share their writing productively. Establishing the classroom conditions you want in the response groups provides the necessary flexibility in varying the composition of small groups throughout a school term. Some activities, for example, work better with pairs, others with groups of three, four, or five members. Sometimes the writing topic should determine who is in which group; sometimes, the students themselves should decide.

The literature on groups isn't particularly convincing in arguing for one size group or another. What seems more apparent is that *some* sizes are better for *some* tasks. Pairs, for example, succeed in carrying out introductory tasks, when students are shy with each other or insecure in collaborative work. Odd numbers, three or five, serve to stimulate discussion and mediate potential controversy because they tend to keep factions of equal size from reaching a standoff. Groups as large as six or more are not easily self-governing and can bury a quiet member, but even as many as 10 students—if they have some experience in group work—can collaborate successfully on projects in which tasks need to be parceled out. None of these variations can succeed, however, without the members of the class as a whole being accustomed to working with each other in different combinations.

What determines effective group composition is the nature of the task, the nature of the students, and the teacher's goals for both group and writing development—not the number itself. Variations in group composition also make it simpler to correct problems as they occur. Without seeming punitive or accusatory, you can shift members from group to group to find more functional combinations of individual personalities. Generally, a mix of sexes, capabilities, and backgrounds is useful in groups, along with a mix of aggressive and compliant members, but there are no failsafe formulas for composing a group. A single aggressive member can tyrannize the rest; a very intelligent student can feel exploited in a group with weaker students; a sexually balanced group can fall into traditional stereotypes of male dominance/female submission. For every "rule" of group composition, there are worrisome exceptions.

The key to establishing and maintaining successful groups is flexibility, because with it comes an openness to experimentation and risk-taking essential not just for students working in groups but for the teachers who work behind them. You may be lucky in assigning students to groups that are productive from the start, or your students may be able to self-select their groups to build on the strengths of existing friendships without bogging down with the obvious drawbacks of these relationships. If so, keep such groups together as long as they are productive. Otherwise, shuffle groupings from one meeting to the next, or ask the students to shuffle themselves, or, time permitting, see if the groups can confront their own shortcomings as they arise and resolve them. These flexible and varied groupings are possible when members of the whole class are familiar with each other. The activities that follow help students get acquainted with each other in both large and small groups.

A. Name Chain

In any group, participants need to know each other's names. Begin your class with a name chain in which a student sitting to your immediate right or left (preferably with the whole class in a circle) introduces herself giving her first name only. The next person introduces himself and then the first person; the third person introduces herself, then the second and first persons, and so on around the circle. Discourage enterprising students from simply keeping a list of names and reading it off. By introducing yourself last, you can usually learn almost everyone's name, a gesture that students appreciate greatly. More important is the fact that in classes larger than 20 very few people can remember all the names, so students will naturally begin helping each other as they share and enjoy their own and each other's lapses of memory. This is a low-risk exercise for students of any age that accomplishes an essential goal in moving the class toward collaborative relations.

B. Self-Disclosure

Self-disclosure exercises accomplish a transition from large to small groups, allowing members to learn something more substantive about their peers and to begin practicing interaction skills in questioning, listening, and speaking that will be further developed later. Ranging in risk from mild to moderate, they can be adjusted according to your students' capabilities.

1. World Traveler

Ask group members to tell each other where they would go if they could take a trip anywhere in the world, how long they would stay, and why they would choose that place. This is a relatively safe exercise that can also be used in the large group by dividing it in half and putting each half in a circle, one inside the other. Moving in counter-rotation each student in the inside circle will meet each student in the outside circle, and they can exchange answers. A follow-up discussion with the whole class will give additional purpose to the exercise and help your students develop a sense of solidarity as a class. Take a poll of the places students have named and develop categories of places and reasons for wanting to go there.

2. Backgrounds and Interests

Ask each member to tell the group something about himself or herself that the others would need to know to become well acquainted. This exercise can either be open ended or can focus on specific areas: sports, hobbies, families, etc. Obviously, the more open-ended the question, the more you risk students' finding nothing to say or fearing that they must disclose something very personal.

3. Interviewer

Divide each small group into pairs and give the pairs 10–20 minutes to find out as much as they can about each other. Ask the interviewer to play the role of a familiar television interviewer or a local personality. Afterwards, the interviewer should introduce the interviewee to the rest of the group. One slightly more risky and time consuming variation is to ask the interviewers to role play the people they interviewed for the group and then have the real interviewee comment on the performance. If you plan to work frequently with role playing, this variation will help to initiate or reinforce that approach.

C. Movement Exercises

In most classes, students are restricted to their seats. Group-centered learning, on the other hand, requires greater mobility, and students need to become comfortable moving around the classroom. These movement exercises convey metaphorically principles in thinking and verbal interaction that will be further developed in the writing class.

These exercises are most effective with junior or senior high school students, but college writing teachers may find them useful to enliven a particularly stuffy or inhibited group. In any class, the success of all these movement exercises depends upon your willingness to introduce, model, and maintain them as playful but purposeful activities.

1. Mirroring

This is a non-verbal exercise commonly used in acting classes. To begin, students should divide into pairs. Ask one student to begin moving, either by miming a familiar activity like washing dishes or waiting for the bus or by moving abstractly, non-referentially. Without speaking, the other student should mirror his partner's movements, following and reflecting what his partner does. The goal is not only to follow exactly but to become familiar enough with each other so that the partners move together, mirroring each other's motions. As students become increasingly able to anticipate their partners' movements, followers can steal the initiative to become the leader so that leadership is traded back and forth nonverbally. Recall or repeat this exercise when you introduce issues in reflective listening and later in empathic feedback.

2. People Machine

This exercise can be used with groups ranging from about eight to twenty. Explain that the class is going to build a machine; this can be an imaginary machine, or you can specify something familiar like a locomotive or a car engine. Ask one student to volunteer by moving and making the sound appropriate to one part of the machine. Then invite the rest of the students to join in and complete the machine. Students should join as they get a specific idea, but you may need to coach them to get everyone involved. The exercise helps to break down physical barriers among students by eliciting self-disclosure through body language; it also playfully demonstrates the nature of collaborative interaction. At some point, you may want to explore the idea of machine-as-metaphor to further clarify the nature of collaboration; that is, machines function only when all the parts work harmoniously.

Modeling

Secondary school teachers—or college teachers who are able to keep track of their former students from one term to the next—can begin work with response groups by inviting former students to model a group session for a new class. Former students who have become comfortable with response groups and effective respondents are quite valuable in showing how such groups operate. They can be invited to bring a draft of something they are currently working on for another class, or even a completed work from the class they had with you to discuss further revisions. Not only can a demonstration group show new students the actual give-and-take of response groups, participants in a follow-up, question-and-answer session usually provide useful commentary (even testimonials) on why they value the process, what kinds of insecurities they have overcome, and the effect of the response group on their own writing development.

Maintaining the Group

Chapter 2 showed how the maintenance functions of group interaction undergird its ability to accomplish its task. Given this essential feature of group life, peer groups need to incorporate activities that make awareness and practice in sustaining the group a regular part of their work. The preceding chapters on listening and feedback showed that many shortcomings in students' interaction stem from lack of knowledge about how groups maintain themselves, and I suggested methods there for developing this dimension of students' awareness and incorporating it into the writing process. What follows are some additional strategies to increase students' abilities to maintain their response groups and to solve specific interaction problems.

1. Observer

Assign one student the role of observer to watch the group's interaction, make notes, and report to the group after a specific interval. Observers might be asked to concentrate on a specific kind of behavior, such as listening, or to give a general impression of how the group works. Tally sheets or checklists can be used to help the observer (and the group) identify particular behaviors. Figures 1 and 2 provide examples.

Once groups understand specific ways that groups maintain themselves, ask observers simply to record each instance of a group member or the group as a whole engaging in one of the functions listed on the tally sheet. This record can be used to stimulate a short discussion at the end of the writing session to help the group assess its performance. The group must understand, however, that tally sheets are only general indications of group behavior and that they reflect *group,* rather than individual, behavior. In its discussion the

FIGURE 1

Observer Tally Sheet on Listening and Feedback

Group Member	Paraphrasing/ Reflecting	Drawing Out	Connecting	Supporting	Challenging
1.					
2.					
3.					
4.					
5.					
6.					

FIGURE 2

Observer Tally Sheet on Challenging Feedback

Defining terms
Clarifying
Reviewing
Giving Examples
Comparing
Testing Validity
Citing Expectations
Finding Alternatives
Piggybacking Ideas

group needs to be aware of responses they give frequently, but also of any glaring absences of responses that would have improved the discussion.

The use of observers also helps to solve two common group problems: the shy student on the one hand, the aggressive student on the other. Shy students often fail to get involved in discussions because they either don't know how to break in or they feel their contributions are unimportant. Serving as observers gives them a definite role to fulfill and a "space" in which to report—helping them become more functional members by gradually shaping their involvement.

Paradoxically, serving as observer helps to take the aggressive member temporarily out of the group by limiting her function to watching and delaying her participation. Aggressive members dominate groups without recognizing how their dominance impedes the process. Assigning aggressive members to observe allows the other members to develop some interaction skills on their own, often changing the group dynamic in the aggressive member's "absence" while still preserving for that person an important function.

2. Group Evaluation Session

Conclude each writing session with a brief (5-minute) follow-up period devoted to analyzing group performance. Initially convene the whole class to describe, analyze, and evaluate a session, focusing on specific issues and weaving in your own observations of the interaction. As students become more familiar with this process, ask them to conduct their own follow-up discussions. Questions should cover listening, feedback, participation, value of group activity, or proposals for change or improvement. The observer's report in Chapter 6 is a useful model. The group might also be asked to make a line drawing of its communication patterns to understand whether its discussion is evenly distributed among the members or dominated by a single teacher surrogate.

3. Teacher's Role

Limit your own role initially to commenting solely on the group's ability to carry out its task and to offering suggestions for improving performance. It is important to anchor evaluative comments in descriptions and examples of what the students are doing, and to praise what the students are doing well. This role provides a model for student observers and for student-led follow-up sessions. More important, it keeps students from expecting their teachers to fulfill the group's task by solving problems and providing "right" answers. At least initially, you can be more useful guiding group interaction, not contributing to their work in writing. As students become more able to rely on each other, you can begin to participate more fully in discussions of their writing.

4. Coaching

An extension of the observer method is to combine two groups of four or five members each by creating pairs of students. Allow one group to engage in a discussion—pre-writing or revising—while one partner sits behind the other, making notes on his or her performance. See Diagram 1.

DIAGRAM 1

y
x

y x   x y

x
y

Stop the discussion after a 10-minute interval; ask the students seated in the outer circle to coach their partners, and reconvene the discussion so the "trainee" can practice the coach's advice. Later in the discussion or in another discussion, reverse roles and repeat the procedure. This technique helps to emphasize the collaborative role of the coach and to de-emphasize the potentially critical role of the group observer. To introduce this exercise to the class as a whole, allow the rest of the members to observe both the initial discussion and subsequent coaching in what has been called a "fishbowl" arrangement. See Diagram 2.

DIAGRAM 2

```
        z       z       z   z           z
                    y
    z               x
z               y x         x y             z
      y x                       x y   z   z
                                    z
      z           y x       x y
  z               z               z
                x
                y
```

5. Role Playing

Group interaction is affected by the roles members assume, however unconsciously they play these roles. Some roles, such as organizer, harmonizer, mediator, or questioner, are quite helpful to the group; others, such as silent member, interrupter, or monopolizer limit the group's potential. Students can gain insight into their group's interaction—the assumptions and patterns that can govern members' behavior—by playing specific roles during a group session and then analyzing the effect of these roles on group discussion.

To help members focus on the roles that affect groups, write out one role per index card and ask each student to draw a card but to keep the role on the card secret from the rest of the group. Then, in a discussion, ask the students to play the roles they have drawn to see how roles help or hinder the group in accomplishing its task.

6. Achieving Consensus

Groups need to learn when to throttle back from generating ideas and offering alternatives. Eventually they need to assess their output and reach consensus on a single best course of action. While prolific, unfettered thinking should characterize pre-writing group activities, students need more goal-directed interaction as they move toward revising and editing. Less mature students, who are especially liable to be overwhelmed by multiple or contradictory responses, need to learn how to resolve differences of opinion in groups.

Consensus doesn't mean unanimity or group think. It does mean that a group finds a particular solution acceptable, even though an individual acting independently might have chosen another alternative. For writing groups, guided exercises in achieving consensus promote skills in confronting different opinions. Rather than simply dumping those differences on the hapless writer, consensus activities help writers mediate among varied opinions and explore the reasons behind them, perhaps using their differences to reach an unexpected synthesis. Although writers must ultimately make their own decisions about content, argument, style, and so on, consensus exercises help them learn what it means to move toward resolution of the group's varied contributions so they can make informed choices independently.

J. William Pfeiffer and John E. Jones offer the following suggestions for achieving consensus:

1. Members should avoid arguing in an attempt to win as individuals. What is "right" is the best collective judgment of the group as a whole.
2. Conflict about ideas, solutions, predictions, etc. should be viewed as helping rather than hindering consensus.
3. Problems are solved best when individual group members accept responsibility for both listening and contributing, so that everyone is included in the decision.
4. Tension-reducing behaviors can be useful if meaningful conflict is not smoothed over prematurely.
5. Each member is responsible for monitoring the processes through which work gets done and for initiating discussions of process when work is becoming ineffective.
6. The best results flow from a fusion of information, logic, and emotion. Value judgments include members' feelings about the data and about the process of decision-making.
7. Consensus results from group deliberation, not from averaging or majority-rule voting.[1]

Once your students understand these features of consensus, divide the class into groups of five or six students. Present each student with one of the following dilemmas and ask them to decide independently how he or she would resolve the problem. Then, ask them to compare their individual solutions and reach a group decision on which they can agree. Conclude the activity with a follow-up discussion of how the group went about the task and how effective it was in reconciling group needs and individual needs. (Similar dilemmas, no doubt, are common to any teacher's experience and provide a rich vein of additional problem-solving experiences.)

You are a student member of a judicial committee of your college. Your committee hears cases of student misconduct and is charged with reaching a decision on appropriate punishment for the offense. Your powers are broad: you can dismiss the case, issue a letter of reprimand, require offenders to complete a specified number of hours working without compensation for the college at a job your committee can specify, require offenders to undergo a specified number of hours of counseling, put the student on disciplinary probation for a period of time your committee can specify, expel the student from the dorms or from college, or create some other appropriate punishment or combine several punishments. The committee tries to choose punishments that have some prospect of teaching offenders better ways to behave in the college environment.

Case 1:

It's final exam time. Two freshmen, returning to their rooms after a party, discover that someone has removed a fire extinguisher from the wall and sprayed the hall. They pick up the extinguisher and decide to have some fun. When they come upon the nearest door, they burst inside and spray the room, damaging furniture, walls, floors, and possessions. Unfortunately, the occupant of the room is also present—a football player studying with two of his fellow players. Realizing too late that the room isn't empty, the freshmen run away with the three angry football players close behind. A fight ensues— one freshman suffers broken ribs, the other breaks a tooth. Considering both the damage to the room and the danger to the other 100 residents who are now unprotected in the event of a fire, what punishment(s) would your committee impose?

Case 2:

A group of students has been having a party in a dorm room. As the party breaks up, about 2:00 a.m., one student removes all the light bulbs from fixtures in the hallway, leaving it totally dark and dangerous in the event of an emergency. In meeting with the committee the student also admits that he and his friends had been drinking at the party—an infraction of the dorm rule against the possession and consumption of alcohol. What does your committee judge an appropriate response?

Case 3:

A student has accumulated 10 unpaid campus parking tickets. Except for the most recent ones, the others are now old enough that their cost is increasing weekly. The student owes $100. The Parking Service sends the student two certified letters, both of which were signed for by someone at the student's residence, asking him to see the Parking Service Director to arrange payment. Otherwise, his registration will be cancelled and transcripts withheld. The student responds to the second letter but claims not to have received the first. Meeting with the Director, the student claims he can't afford the payments. The Director agrees to reduce the fines to half on half the tickets but reminds the student of a regulation that allows drivers to carry a maximum of 5 unpaid citations. The Director reduces 5 tickets to $10 each and the student agrees to pay. On his way to the cashier, he alters the citations and claims the Director will let him pay $10 for all five tickets to clear up the fine. He pays the $10. In meeting with the judicial committee the student initially denies falsifying the documents, and after eventually admitting to having made the changes he reiterates that he cannot pay the fines. Thus the charges against the student involve failure to pay parking citations, falsifying university documents, and lying to the judicial committee. What punishment does the committee find appropriate and why?

Collaborative Problem Solving

In addition to learning how to achieve consensus, beginning students need experience in solving problems collaboratively. The exercises below take students outside the context of writing. Like stretching exercises before a race, these puzzles help students limber up mental capabilities that are needed for the real thing—writing. The exercises are games that have been widely used to develop problem solving and creative thinking abilities. They pose a range of puzzles sampling perceptual, linguistic, narrative, and intuitive problems. Collectively, they stimulate flexibility in multiple modes of thinking. More important, they evoke self-awareness of these modes of thinking, making the player more able either to apply these modes to subsequent problems or to understand the various kinds of thinking that problem-solving requires.

Each of these games is both an end in itself and a metaphor for a particular thinking skill that is useful in other problem solving situations. The game of "Concealed Colors," for example, illustrates the need to look at a problem from a different perspective and gives the experience of feeling that shift from one perspective to another.

Because these exercises are so obviously metaphors for problem solving, they simulate the experience of resolving the tension of a problem to the fit of a solution. The exercises I've included here teach methods of problem solving experientially by letting students engage in them. The explanation at the beginning of each game balances the experience with a discussion of the thinking process itself: what kinds of abilities the game requires, its value in creative thinking, its relationship to what good problem solvers do, and so on.

Although one can play these games privately, collaboration makes them go faster with less frustration and more success. Individually, most people find they are better at one kind of game than another; collectively they experience the value of shared strengths, solving as a group problems they couldn't solve alone. The games involve players in piggybacking on one another's ideas to generate new ones and eventually to solve the puzzle. In this respect, the games help students overcome shyness at not knowing answers beforehand (the old product mentality) and let them experience the value of collaborative efforts. The metaphorical implications of the games are as important as the experience itself: success in piggybacking ideas to solve puzzles lays the groundwork for fruitful discussion of revision strategies in subsequent writing workshops. Finally, a class period spent playing these games in pairs and small groups can demonstrate to students their real ability to be self-directing: to define both the problems and the procedures for solving puzzles. Followed by a thorough description and analysis of the class period, the games provide a model of successful collaborative learning that can serve as a touchstone for subsequent group activities in writing. To reinforce their connection with writing, develop a writing assignment around this activity. First, ask students to make notes for discussion focused on questions like the following:

What procedures did you and your partner or group use to solve the problem?
What kinds of thinking did you learn about?
How did you know when you had found a solution?
What happened if people disagreed on answers or solutions?
Were you more able to solve one kind of problem than another? Why?
What did you learn about your own thinking?

Use the notes on these questions as the basis for the next day's class, and make it clear that one function of writing is to help people collect and organize experience and to inform discussion. In subsequent assignments, especially pre-writing workshops, help students recall both the processes they engaged in and the thinking skills they learned, or isolate a particular exercise to introduce more deliberate work in specific invention strategies such as brainstorming.

Introduce these games by explaining that they serve the double purpose of teaching (1) invention skills that help writers generate ideas, and (2) helping students learn to work collaboratively, as they will in writing. Be sure that you have already established the collaborative approach to writing you will be using. The students should already be slightly acquainted, although these exercises are good ice-breakers and work well during the first weeks of a term. Have the students pair up, but encourage them to change partners and merge pairs throughout the session. The goal is to achieve maximum ease and flexibility in groupings. Reproduce each exercise on an index card. Distribute one card to each pair, leaving any extras where all students can reach them. Instruct them to work on each card until they have either given up or solved enough of the puzzle to get the gist of it. Then they should exchange cards with another group or get a fresh card from the leftovers. They should continue to exchange cards throughout the period, working with a wide variety of puzzles and keeping track of the array of thinking skills and perceptual problems each one introduces. If you choose to follow the exercise with the writing assignment described above, introduce it at this point. You will also need to assure students that this is not a test, and you can probably do this best by drifting from group to group, engaging in the problem-solving process with them. (I have withheld solutions to these puzzles to affirm that the process in this activity is more important than the product.)

Exercises in Creativity and Problem Solving[2]

1. Concealed Colors

This puzzle shows you how we limit our perceptions by habit. We see according to familiar boundaries, yet we need to achieve the flexibility to break out of those boundaries. See how many hidden colors your group can find in the sentences below.

Example: The cab lacked the proper brakes to stop at the intersection.

Answer: Black

1. A big *old* hungry dog appeared at our door every morning.
2. The cop persuaded him not to create a disturbance.
3. The Brazilian student Paulo lives just around the corner from us.
4. You shouldn't let an upstart like him bother you.
5. LaJolla venders decided to cut their prices in half.
6. Long rayon fabrics were loaded on the truck.
7. The new law hit everybody's pocketbook pretty hard.
8. The kitten chased the big pear lying near the tree.
9. You can always catch Rome on your way back from Naples.
10. No one thought of awnings to protect the merchandise from the sun.
11. To build up your chest, nutrients derived from milk products are the best.
12. Bob's car let out dark fumes when he tried to drive it up the steep hill.

2. STARS

Good writers enjoy playing with words and they are fluent in trying out many alternatives even if some are nonsensical. See how many sentences you and your partners can produce using each letter in **STARS** as the first letter of each word in the sentence. Use each other's ideas to build the sentences, and see if you get better at producing sentences as you go along.

Example: *S*oft *t*ires *a*re *r*eal *s*cary.

3. Resourceful Alternatives

Creative thinkers are able to go beyond stereotyped, habitual responses and traditional values. They think of many alternatives or solutions to problems before choosing one. In this game, see how many outcomes your group can imagine, trying not only for commonplace suggestions but original and imaginative ones as well.

What would happen if there were no traffic laws?

4. Brainstorming

The most widely used method of coming up with ideas in groups is brainstorming. There are only four rules:

1. You're initially after quantity not quality: generate as many ideas as possible.
2. Group members may not evaluate any idea until all are in; the key is to overcome the inhibitions that can hamper creativity.
3. Unusual, even crazy ideas are encouraged: sometimes, upon reflection, the silliest idea can be modified to produce the best solution to a problem.
4. Group members should try to piggyback on each other's ideas, using one idea to elicit another either by modification or association.

Problem: A brickyard is faced with an over-supply of bricks. Since it cannot afford to keep them stockpiled, the company must get rid of them quickly. Think of as many uses as you can for bricks so the company can devise an advertising campaign that will attract new customers. (Hint: Don't limit your thinking to the conventional uses of bricks; consider their potential uses based on properties such as size, color, and weight.)

5. This exercise stimulates your fluency with words and helps you overcome perceptual boundaries. Create sentences that hide the following household items:

chair	sink	plate	bed
table	lamp	glass	blanket
candle	shelf	fork	window

Example: John al*so fa*res well in math.

6. Perceiving Relations

New ideas often come from seeing a relationship between elements that would at first seem unrelated. Clear group discussion and clear writing both depend on perceiving and expressing those relationships. This exercise provides practice in forming the associations that lead to new ideas and clear expression.

Think of a fifth word related to the preceeding four words. You can form compounds, hyphenated words, and commonly used expressions.

Examples:

Elephant	bleed	lie	wash	(white)
white elephant		bleed white	whitewash	white lie
Sleeping	contest	spot	shop	(beauty)
Style	love	jacket	span	(life)

Bug	Rest	Fellow	Caves
Cross	Baby	Blood	Ribbon
See	Carpet	Hot	Cent
Touch	Palate	Soap	Sell
Easy	Hush	Belt	Order
Tree	Cup	Cake	Forbidden
Wagon	Stand	Aid	Dance
Dust	Movie	Gaze	Sapphire
Tooth	Talk	Potato	Bitter
Alley	Date	Snow	Spot
Call	Nap	Burglar	Hep
Rest	Post	Linen	Fellow
Bulldog	Cuff	Toast	Windows
Opera	No	Box	Stone
Brain	Watching	Bath	House
Wire	Out	Feed	Play

7. Kinships and Associations

Creative people have described their thought processes as associative. As the mathematician Jules Poincare said, "to create consists of making new combinations of associative elements . . . The mathematical facts worthy of being studied are those which reveal to us unsuspected kinships between other facts well known but wrongly believed to be strangers to one another."

Think of a word that precedes those in the first two columns and follows those in the last two. You can form compounds, hyphenated words, common expressions, colloquial usage or slang.

Example:

Break	Strings	<u>Heart</u>	Purple	Take
Sell	Rock	<u>Hard</u>	Work	Hit
Rate	Account	_____	Savings	Left
Salad	Head	_____	Lay	Rotten
Corner	Rope	_____	Sit	Hold
Opera	House	_____	Flash	Flood
Artist	Clause	_____	Narrow	Fire
Dog	Skin	_____	Herds	Count
In	Ugly	_____	Spark	Drain
Ox	Bunny	_____	Deaf	Strike
Backer	Drawing	_____	Fishing	Telephone
Shooting	Door	_____	Shut	Tourist
Ware	Foot	_____	Fall	A
Step	Flesh	_____	Wild	Cook
Die	Cart	_____	Rotten	Crab
Air	Tub	_____	Get	Boiling
Rage	Look	_____	Wash	Reach
Day	Theory	_____	Magnetic	Playing

8. Tardy Student

People's success in solving problems is limited by the number of solutions they can devise. People who can generate many potential solutions usually do so because they can see the problem from many angles.

Try to come up with as many solutions as possible for this real life problem: If you were a teacher and the best student in your class was constantly late getting to school in the morning, what might you do to correct his or her lateness?

9. The Frugal Woman

Successful problem solvers are able to think of many different explanations for what they observe. Only after they have amassed as many explanations as they can do they subject them to test or critical analysis to arrive at the best or most likely explanation.

Less creative problem solvers tend to be mentally impatient. They stick to the first likely explanation that occurs and rest content with it. The generation of hypotheses—or ideas—is a crucial part of problem analysis, for the simple reason that we can't evaluate an explanation that hasn't occurred to us.

A woman changes her frugal habits and spends money very freely. How many prior circumstances can you suggest to account for this? List as many ideas as you can.

10. Sound and Meaning

Effective writers are not just concerned with the meaning they wish to convey; they also consider the sound of words and the rhythm of phrases. They play around with language to achieve the right blend of sound and meaning.

This game exercises your ability to produce complete sentences that repeat the same sound. Choose a letter of the alphabet and in a five-minute interval write as many sentences as you can in which each word begins with that letter.

Example: T — Tea tastes terrific.

11. Common Denominators

Creative thinking frequently depends on the ability to see similarities and differences between entities or objects. Sometimes it is a single link not immediately apparent that relates several otherwise dissimilar things. It may be an attribute like "whiteness" that links a polar bear and a potato, or a function like the ability to provide shade and shelter that links a tree and an umbrella. Inventive people have learned to make these associations very rapidly.

Select the one word that does not belong:

Example: canoe, log, engine, ship, raft

Answer: engine — all others float

Motorcycle, carnage, car, boat, train
Boxing, skating, ping-pong, wrestling, football
Peanut, carrot, stringbean, potato, radish
Coward, mean, honest, rich, loyal
Far, fifteen, twenty, six, twenty-two
Sculpture, painting, mobile, monument, bas-relief
Fantasy, fancy, idea, vision, reverie
Abasement, humiliation, criticism, disgrace, dishonor
Television, book, radio, magazine, game
Lion, hyena, giraffe, bear, wolf
Oak, weeping willow, maple, mahogany, pine

12. Word Chains

Most creative people are noted for the voluminous vocabulary they have at their command. The more words you can think of the more readily you can form associations. Words represent ideas, and most creative new ideas are the result of a thinking process called association of ideas. By exercising your vocabulary, you increase your power to identify, associate, and relate ideas.

Here is a series of four-letter words that have nothing in common. By changing only one letter at a time, think of a series of words to build a bridge between the two. The fewer words you use the better.

Example: Work/lame

Work pork pore tore tome tame lame
Work wore lore lare lame

Fire/Mint
Lore/Part
Rise/Bath
Hale/Lore
Next/Mean
Swim/Clip
Give/Take
Tour/Sort
Male/Word
Miss/Base
Cake/Bill
Mean/Soap
Pave/Tort
Wild/More
Book/List
Came/Dirt

13. Metaphorical Thinking

Similes and metaphors are figures of speech that aren't limited to poetry. They are effective methods of showing similarities between things not usually considered similar. They help readers visualize and understand abstract or difficult ideas in terms of concrete, familiar experiences.

Complete the following similes, and try more than one approach:

Example: Money is like promises —

Possible answer: easier made than kept.

Wishes, like castles in the air,
Time is like money
The world is like a great staircase
Money is like manure
A woman, like a melon,
Advice is like kissing
Truth shines like the sun
Prejudice, like the spider,
Love, like a cough,

14. Pairs

Creative people tend to form clear, sharp impressions of things they observe. As a result, the accumulated information in their memory storage is substantial. And they can easily retrieve the needed information when called upon to do so. Readily recallable information is essential for creative and flexible thinking.

List all the things you can think of that come in pairs.

15. Connect the Dots

Thinking often becomes constrained by the limitations or boundaries people impose on problems. Your ability to solve this problem comes from your ability to see beyond the apparent boundaries.

Connect the dots with four lines, drawn without lifting the pencil from the paper.

```
•   •   •

•   •   •

•   •   •
```

Recording Peer Input

Groups most frequently fail to carry out tasks when the task is entirely open-ended and no tangible outcome is expected. Similarly, writers often fail (1) to formulate their own questions for groups to consider, and (2) to put their peers' responses to good use. Providing note sheets for each phase of the review process and requiring that these sheets be turned in with the final revision helps students to monitor the evolution of texts and to become accountable for the productive outcome of each review session. Here are examples of three guides to take students through pre-writing, reviewing a draft, and revising, at each step asking them to compare their initial thinking with the input they receive from peers and to summarize their next steps. In a workshop on a one-page assignment, instruct students to allow about 10 minutes for each person to present ideas or a draft, and keep them within these time limits.

A. Peer Response Guide for Pre-Writing

Before the Group Session	*After the Group Session*
I. Prior to the group session summarize in one or two sentences your purpose for this piece of writing and the plans you have to carry it out.	III. List the most useful contributions of your group from this session.

II. List the key ideas you plan to include in your paper.

IV. Write one or two sentences summarizing the approach you now plan to take in drafting your paper.

B. Peer Response Guide for Reviewing Drafts

Before the Group Session	*After the Group Session*
I. Prior to the group session, note what you believe are the strengths of this draft (what do you particularly like? What are its best ideas?).	III. Summarize the most essential contributions of your group.

II. Note the sticking points (what are you still unsure about? What are its weaknesses?).

IV. List the modifications you plan to make in the draft.

C. Peer Response Guide for Revising

Before the Group Session

I. Describe the present status of your text.

_____
_____
_____

II. Note the questions you have for the group to consider.

_____
_____
_____

After the Group Session

III. List the adjustments you need to make for the final revision.

_____
_____
_____

These techniques, and others they may suggest, are more than distractions from the central task of teaching writing. Rather, they develop the skills essential to writing in the interpersonal context that is most like its actual practice outside the writing class. To the extent that this communal context influences the how and why of writing, students must learn more than isolated composing skills. They need to learn how to analyze texts and discuss them with others. Moreover, as this chapter and others have argued, this broad interpersonal context stimulates a broad range of cognitive, social, and linguistic abilities. Writing is but one dimension of these interrelated skills.

None of these exercises is foolproof. And certainly no one would want to use all of them. Many should be modified to suit a particular teaching style or situation. Together, however, they represent a commitment to the value of developing strategies for collaborative learning and a willingness to teach writing not just as a basic skill but as a process of exploring and representing ideas. Sharing writing, like writing itself, is an essential part of the dialectic of social interaction.

Notes

1.   J. William Pfeiffer and John E. Jones, eds., *Handbook of Structured Group Experiences for Human Relations Training*, Volumes 2 and 7, San Diego, California: University Associates.
2.   From CREATIVE GROWTH GAMES copyright Eugene Raudsepp and George P. Hughs, Jr. 1977. The Berkley Publishing Group.